CLASSIC WALKS IN THE
Peak District
by Martin Collins

The Oxford Illustrated Press

FOR PAUL

Thanks are due to many people whose interest, hospitality, advice and encouragement over a number of years paved the way for this book. I am especially grateful to Diana for precious memories of innumerable shared walks in the Peak District and for her patience during the preparation of the manuscript and illustrations.

All photographs and maps by the author.

©1991, Martin Collins

ISBN 1 85509 215 8

Published by: The Oxford Illustrated Press, Haynes Publishing Group, Sparkford, Nr Yeovil, Somerset BA22 7JJ, England

Printed in England by: J.H. Haynes & Co Limited, Sparkford, Nr Yeovil, Somerset

British Library Cataloguing in Publication Data:
Collins, Martin *1941-*
   Classic walks in the Peak District. - (Classic walks series)
   1. Derbyshire (England)
   I. Title II. Series
   914.251104859

   ISBN 1-85509-215-8

Library of Congress Catalog Card Number: 91-71106

Contents

The Peak District National Park   4
   Landscapes of the Peak
   Walking Gear and Safety on the Hills
   About the Walks

Walk 1:   Villages at the Southern Gateway   11
Walk 2:   Grindon, Musden Wood and Beeston Tor   15
Walk 3:   Dove Dale   19
Walk 4:   Parwich, The Tissington Trail and Eaton Dale   23
Walk 5:   Thor's Cave, The Manifold Valley and Ecton Copper Mines   26
Walk 6:   The Roystone Grange Archaeological Trail   30
Walk 7:   Four Dales from Hartington   34
Walk 8:   Limestone Peaks of the Upper Dove Valley   38
Walk 9:   The Roaches, Lud's Church and Hen Cloud   42
Walk 10:   Arbor Low, Bradford Dale and the High Peak Trail   45
Walk 11:   Moneyash, Lathkill Dale and Youlgreave   49
Walk 12:   Bakewell and Haddon Hall   54
Walk 13:   Dales and Villages from Monsal Head   57
Walk 14:   Chatsworth Park   61
Walk 15:   The Monsal Trail and Chee Dale   64
Walk 16:   The South Eastern Gritstone Edges   67
Walk 17:   Villages and Moors around Eyam   71
Walk 18:   Shining Tor and the Goyt Valley   76
Walk 19:   Hathersage Moor, Longshaw Park and Padley Gorge   79

Walk 20:   Hathersage and Stanage Edge   82
Walk 21:   Castleton, Mam Tor, and the Show Caves   85
Walk 22:   Lose Hill, Win Hill and the Vale of Edale   89
Walk 23:   The Great Ridge   92
Walk 24:   A Circuit of Edale Head   95
Walk 25:   Edale and a Circuit of Grindsbrook Clough   98
Walk 26:   The Kinder Edges   101
Walk 27:   Derwent Edge, Abbey Brook and the Reservoirs   105
Walk 28:   The Snake Path   109
Walk 29   Alport Castles, Derwent Dale and the Woodlands Valley   111
Walk 30:   Bleaklow Head from Old Glossop   114
Walk 31:   The Howden Moors and River Derwent   118
Walk 32:   Black Hill and Laddow Rocks   121

Four Railway Trails   124
   The Tissington Trail
   The High Peak Trail
   The Monsal Trail
   The Manifold Track

Long Distance Walks   127
   The Derwent Watershed
   Marsden to Edale
   The Eastern Gritstone Edges
   The Limestone Way

Useful Addresses   135

A Country Code for The Peak District   136

The Peak District National Park

If you glance at a map of England you will notice, roughly in the middle, an oval shape ringed by motorways and the industrial conurbations of Sheffield, Derby, The Potteries, Manchester and Huddersfield. Unlikely though it may seem, this relatively small enclave—the Peak District National Park—contains some of the wildest and loveliest countryside in Britain. Its value as an amenity is immense—some 20 million people visit it each year—yet paradoxically the general public has not always been welcome here.

Following World War I, and especially during the Depression years, these moors and dales represented a release from grime and drudgery for countless thousands of city dwellers who flocked out by train at every opportunity to enjoy a few precious hours of freedom in the hills. Wide horizons, the challenge of physical exertion, walking alone or in the easy company of friends come rain or shine, all helped to counterbalance lives otherwise spent in confined and often squalid surroundings. In 1926 John Derry, that standard-bearer of the early rambling movement, crystallised prevailing sentiments in his guidebook *Across the Derbyshire Moors:* 'And yet it does one good to get into this upland, age-long solitude, where the primeval world is felt to be a mighty fact, linked on to us.'

There were, however, considerable obstacles to be surmounted in those pre-National Park days. Land was (as it still is) mainly in private ownership and in order to protect their grouse-shooting income, landowners barred ramblers from vast tracts of Kinder Scout, Bleaklow and the eastern moors. 'Trespassers will be Prosecuted' boards were erected (dubbed 'wooden liars' because trespass, of course, is not a prosecutable offence) and armed gamekeepers were posted at strategic access points.

Understandably, resentment boiled up when ramblers confronted such restrictions on their 'right to roam'. Ugly scenes erupted, rewards were offered in local newspapers for the identification of photographed trespassers, and the more militant ramblers regularly risked spells of imprisonment for their passionately held cause. To quote John Derry again: 'Nothing keeps alive the spirit of revolt and iconoclasm so fiercely as a refusal to the general community of the use of their eyes over beautiful remote tracts of the earth, under the plea of private ownership.'

Unemployment and the emergence of polit-ical awareness among working class people during the 1920s and early 1930s lent momentum to the access movement. Mass protest rallies held near Castleton expressed a common desire for free access to crags and moorland—a call which would echo ever louder down the ensuing decades.

Everything came to a head with the famous Mass Trespass of 24th April 1932, in which some 400 ramblers set off from Hayfield, their sights set firmly on reaching the forbidden Kinder Scout plateau and forcing a confrontation with the landowners. The event had been well publicised beforehand so they were met below the plateau edge at Sandy Heys by groups of keepers. With emotions running high, verbal exchanges inevitably escalated to physical scuffles, as a result of which 6 ramblers were given jail sentences of between 2 and 6 months for assault and riotous assembly.

Not everyone was convinced that the Kinder Trespass, and others which followed in its wake, were either necessary or effective since access concessions were not won for a number of years. However, there can be little doubt that these manifestations of public defiance against the landowning aristocracy spearheaded a steady shift towards recognition that the countryside should be there for all to enjoy. By 1949 this concept had become enshrined in the National Parks and Access to the Countryside Act; two years later the Peak District was established as Britain's first National Park.

Access had never been problematic in the cultivated White Peak, with its matrix of ancient field and riverside paths, but agreements still had to be hammered out with Dark Peak landowners: today some 76 square miles (197 square km) of the northern and eastern moors are designated 'Open Country' (except for a number of days during the grouse-shooting season between 12th August and 10th December).

Water Authorities, too, have relaxed their attitudes to the leisure use of water-gathering grounds, though sensible rules to prevent pollution still apply. Other landowners include the National Trust and the Park Authorities themselves. It is worth remembering that, unlike National Parks which in America and many other countries are state-owned, those in Britain belong to the same mixture of private individuals and public bodies as exists outside the National Parks.

It is said that half the population of England lives within a 60 mile (95km) radius of Buxton—about 17 million people. The pronouncement by Sir Arthur Hobhouse in his report on National Parks to the post-World War II Labour government that the Peak District's '. . . very proximity to the industrial towns render it as vulnerable as it is valuable' has never rung more true. Pressures on our 10 National Parks continue to grow; indeed, as I write, a review of their present condition is under way. Commentators are suggesting that these areas of beautiful and relatively wild country, protected as part of our national heritage and funded largely by central government, may have insufficient resources to deal with the unprecedented interest shown in them by a public attracted to outdoor activities and all things 'natural'.

But the onslaught comes from other directions too. In the Peak Park, valleys have been flooded for reservoirs, the dark huddle of conifers shrouds many a hillside, new roads and buildings creep outwards from existing suburbs, while cottages and farmhouses by the hundred are converted into holiday or second homes.

An even greater threat is posed by the continuing extraction of minerals such as fluorspar and limestone which creates noise, dust, mud and heavy traffic—a thorn in the side of the Peak Park authorities whose brief to preserve characteristic landscape beauty carefully is made all the harder to implement. In his book *The National Parks of England and Wales* (Oxford Illustrated Press), Brian Redhead declares: 'What is quarrying but the authorised removal of a Park? Once you have dug out a chunk, you cannot say that you are sorry and that you will put it back again. There should be no question of quarrying in the Parks for minerals that can be found elsewhere.' At least the areas around New Mills, Whaley Bridge, Chapel-en-le-Frith and Buxton are excluded from the National Park, whose boundary forms a long indentation to avoid the greatest concentrations of industrial and quarrying activity; Matlock and Darley Dale are similarly omitted.

Since 1968 the Countryside Commission has assumed overall responsibility for our National Parks, each one of which is administered by a local government authority—in this case the Peak Park Joint Planning Board. Of its 34 members, 23 represent those local and district councils with territory in the Park, while 11 are appointed by the Secretary of State for the Environment to look after national interests and for their ability to contribute special expertise.

The Joint Planning Board addresses itself to providing amenities and services for the public within the Park (such as the Ranger Service and Information Centres), to making planning decisions, and to devising schemes which promote both conservation of the environment and the successful operation of the Park in its dual role as workplace and a major tourist destination. Central government grant support accounts for about 75% of the Peak Park's funding, the remainder coming from its own income-generating activities and from the local Community Charge.

Landscapes of The Peak

It will quickly become apparent to newcomers that there are no 'peaks' in the Peak District, nor one culminating summit that could claim 'peak' status! In fact, the name derives from an Old English word 'Peac', denoting a hill or knoll.

The National Park's 542 square miles (1404 square kms) contain two distinct types of scenery: the White Peak and the Dark (or High) Peak. Variations in the region's geology are responsible, not only influencing land forms, patterns of human settlement, flora and fauna, but also providing very different kinds of walking experiences. Despite years of tramping the Derbyshire hills, I am still struck by this dichotomy. On a south-to-north hike you can be threading intimate dales flanked by flowery hillsides and limestone crags, then, within a span of 5 or 6 miles (8.5km), rising to 2000ft (610m) onto sombre moors overlaid by a hostile wilderness of bog and peat hags.

The transition from White to Dark Peak (wholly appropriate descriptive names) is that of limestone to millstone grit, each supporting a distinctive landscape. The Park's southern limestone heartland is predominantly agricultural, a soft and fertile place characterised by the slow, ubiquitous march of drystone walls; grazing cattle and sheep; villages and farmsteads of pale stone; tree-topped hills and steep-sided, rocky dales. This is the northern threshold of lowland Britain, many of whose plant and animal species are well represented.

Geologically speaking, limestone is the accretion of skeletons from countless millions of tiny crustaceans and was formed, in this case, during the Carboniferous Period some 330 million years ago. Conical eminences such as Thorpe Cloud and Parkhouse Hill represent the vestiges of coral reefs, also laid down in that far-off, warm, tropical sea.

Subsequent volcanic action introduced deposits of silica sand, basalt, copper and lead, all of which—together with the limestone

Hartington—a popular village with walkers at the heart of the White Peak.

itself—have been subject to extraction by mining and quarrying. In some locations the landscape continues to suffer the consequences of mineral exploitation, but elsewhere the relics of those old industries reward us with insights into the lives and technologies of our forebears.

Following an uplifting of the region into a vast dome, gritstones and shales overlying the ancient limestone were eroded away by natural forces, exposing the bleached bones of the earth, still flanked to the north, west and east by younger beds of millstone grit. Deep, picturesque dales, for which the White Peak is perhaps best loved, were probably carved into the plateau by torrents of glacial meltwater towards the end of the last Ice Age, though the picture is complex and other factors may well have been involved. The features we admire today—extraordinary limestone formations and caverns, dry river beds whose water flows underground, bold crags beloved of rock-climbers, and the often wooded slopes of winding gorges—all have an enormous capacity to attract and intrigue visitors. Indeed, as John Ruskin once declared; 'The whole gift of the country is in its glens . . . it is only in the clefts of it, and the dingles, that the traveller finds

his joy.' In places like Dovedale, modern day sightseers threaten to overwhelm the natural environment, but as readers of this book will discover, opportunities for exploring off the beaten track are legion.

Since early man first occupied cave shelters here, these limestone uplands and dales have become the chosen land for human settlement. Stone circles, Bronze Age burial mounds, long-abandoned earthworks and cultivation terraces predate recorded history, but by the Middle Ages open field farming had been established and the Enclosure Acts of 1760–1830 gave birth to the matrix of drystone walling—hallmark of the White Peak landscape. Today's villages, increasingly colonised by commuters and holidaymakers, still retain links with their past through customs such as well-dressing, wakes, the Castleton Garland and many others.

Walking in the White Peak is infinitely varied and utterly delightful in most weathers, though the prevailing altitude—around

5

1000–1500ft (300–460m)— can produce harsh conditions in winter. Shelter is usually available and civilisation is never far away. If you enjoy a drink or a snack along the way, a pub or cafe can often be built into your itinerary, and a web of minor roads facilitates the organisation of lifts. Other than on main roads, however, bus services are sketchy and the White Peak is not served by convenient railway stations. Bakewell ranks as the White Peak's largest town within the National Park boundary, but Buxton, Ashbourne, Matlock and many smaller villages all have much to offer the visitor.

Millstone grit is a coarse-textured, blackish-brown rock. It caps the shales and sandstones in the Peak's northern sector and curves south in a great horseshoe to embrace both sides of the White Peak. Acidic and often poorly drained, the Dark Peak soil discourages cultivation except in some valley pockets, so sheep form the mainstay of hill farming. The most widely encountered varieties will be the hornless Derbyshire Gritstone, the black-faced Swaledale and even the once-rare Jacobs breed—all hardy, self-sufficient animals; Clun Forest and Suffolk dominate the lower slopes.

Apart from populations of curlew, plover, foxes and mountain hare, sheep share these bleak moors with only one other species: red grouse. For years earlier this century, grouse-shooting kept wild country permanently out of bounds to the general public, leading to the Kinder Trespasses as discussed earlier. Even today the 'sport' is indulged from the 'Glorious Twelfth' of August to 10th December, closing off sections of moor for a few days at a time. In order to encourage the growth of tender new shoots upon which grouse feed, heather is periodically burnt back, some denser patches being left for nesting cover.

From Black Hill south to Kinder Scout, peat predominates! Thousands of acres of dissected dark-brown wilderness are relieved only by the occasional swath of cotton grass or hare's tail—plants just able to cling to the margin of life! Original woodlands of elm, oak and lime which once clothed these expansive tops fostered areas of sphagnum moss in boggy hollows, but it was tree clearance by Neolithic communities—the first farmers—along with grazing by animals which set in train the depletion and eventual disappearance of those early forests. Without the consolidating and regenerative effects of tree cover, the land lay waste and vegetation rotted to form the thick peat layer so characteristic of the Dark Peak today. Writing in his *Pennine Way Companion*, that doyen of hillwalkers Alfred Wainwright, describes the moors east of Bleaklow Head as 'an inhospitable wilderness of peat bogs over

which progress on foot is very arduous.' Before him, Daniel Defoe had declared the Peak 'the most desolate, wild and abandoned country in England.'

Happily there is another, more appealing, aspect to the Dark Peak landscape. Outcroppings of millstone grit have been sculpted by wind and weather into spectacular shapes on the moortops, and form fringes of precipitous crags where the high ground drops to valleys, or 'cloughs'. Particularly down the eastern arm of the gritstone 'horseshoe', these edges are a striking feature. Many significant developments in British rock climbing took place on the walls and buttresses, and they remain a mecca for climbers of all abilities. The rock itself was in great demand for millstones around which a thriving industry grew until technical innovations rendered them obsolete in the mid-nineteenth century.

Though less pastoral in intent, the hand of man has been as instrumental in shaping the landscape of the Dark Peak as of the White Peak. With roots in the Industrial Revolution, huddled settlements of blackened stone strike an altogether more subdued, even disconsolate, note. In sheer scale and environmental impact, however, they are surpassed by the flooding of valleys as reservoirs to satisfy the thirst of adjacent cities, and by the afforestation of hillsides with alien conifers.

Hiking in the Dark Peak, with its wide horizons and challenging terrain, is both exhilarating and rather more serious than in the limestone country further south—though much depends on the weather and choice of routes. Walking the eastern gritstone edges, for example, is a treat suitable for the whole family, but edges further north and east entail traversing remoter country.

The Edale valley excepted, it is perhaps the relative scarcity of human habitation—let alone refreshment places!—that adds spice to Dark Peak outings. Here, at 2000ft (610m), survival for any living creature can be tough. Annual rainfall totals over 60″ (1520mm); gales and damp, clinging mists, as on all Britain's hills, are not uncommon, and snow transforms the moors into inhospitable semi-tundra. You are, to a much greater extent, on your own, and in the interests of safety should go properly equipped and able to use a map and compass. Negotiating peat drainage channels ('groughs') and their overhanging banks ('hags')—a strenuous pastime otherwise known as 'bog-trotting'—should not be attempted by novice hillwalkers. The rewards to be gained are, of course, commensurate and there is great satisfaction in discovering one of Britain's true wildernesses, albeit one of modest size.

Three trunk roads cross the Dark Peak, and

while buses do serve neighbouring communities, private transport is frequently the most useful method of reaching a walk's starting point. Exceptions are those routes lying near stations on British Rail's Sheffield to Manchester line via the Edale valley, Edale itself being the principal Dark Peak centre.

Walking Gear and Safety on The Hills

The great joy of British weather lies in its variability: how fortunate we are to witness the raw moods of nature, from storm to heatwave, mist to gale, ice, snow and rain to interludes of drought. Yet this very changeability means that in hill country we need to protect ourselves against the elements, not only to ensure our comfort but sometimes survival itself.

The reason, of course, is the body's requirement to maintain a steady temperature as well as a healthy balance of fluids and energy-producing nutrients. Lower or raise our core temperature by just a few degrees and life is threatened; deprive our system of water or food and it eventually refuses to respond to physical demands. In everyday life we seldom give more than a passing moment's thought to this continuous balancing act—according to the season we simply wear heavier or lighter clothing and have developed numerous strategies for warming up or cooling off. Travelling in the sheltered cocoon of car, bus or train removes us from direct contact with the environment, while taking in adequate food and drink simply constitutes part of our daily routine.

When hillwalking (other than on short, easy routes) the situation differs in several respects. Trudging over rough ground and climbing substantial gradients burns up many more calories than walking over flat, even terrain. Add the weight of a rucksack, boots and outdoor clothing, perhaps a camera and other odds and ends, and you may need to increase your daily calorie intake by up to 50%.

If nibbled regularly, trail snacks such as chocolate, raisins, muesli bars etc will lighten your step between halts for a more sustaining pub meal or picnic. However, no amount of sensible eating will prevent fatigue from setting in when your body's ability to convert its fuel (oxygen, water, food) into energy begins to break down. Only a programme of aerobic exercise—jogging, swimming, cycling or hard walking—will push back your threshold of endurance and thus increase the range of walks you will be able to undertake.

Strenuous physical exertion also depletes the body's fluid reserves through sweating and

The Kinder plateau (above) and the
Hallam Moors (right). During
prolonged dry weather the risk of fire
is considerable.

The Vale of Edale in winter
conditions.

evaporation when breathing. Although summertime heat presents the most obvious scenario for this, climbing hills in any season can induce sweating. Unless you are assured of passing a cafe or pub,. it is generally prudent to carry a drink of some kind; a thermos flask will keep it hot or cool depending on the time of year and prevailing weather.

Especially on extended hikes, cold weather exacerbated by strong winds with rain or snow (the wind-chill factor) makes further inroads into energy reserves, creating conditions in which a natural appetite—the normally reliable index of hunger—may be suppressed. Indeed, in hostile weather just keeping warm uses up energy, increasing the need to protect the body from heat loss. This is best achieved by wearing several thin layers of warm clothing under a windproof/waterproof 'shell' of cagoule and overtrousers—a much more versatile arrangement than one thick, heavy sweater or jacket. Breathable fabrics (such as Goretex) prevent the build up of condensation inside the outer garments. They are, however, expensive, so unless you intend doing a lot of serious walking cheaper alternatives will suffice.

Fibre pile garments are cosy to wear, even when wet, as are lightweight vests, shirts and jackets made from modern fabrics which are both warm and which 'wick' perspiration away from the skin. Again, the cost can be high and perfectly good service will be obtained from ordinary underwear, cotton or wool shirts and wool jumpers.

It should not be forgotten that our heads act like radiators, rapidly dispersing heat if left uncovered in cold or wet conditions. Most cagoules have a hood, but a woolly hat (in winter a balaclava) provides additional insulation. Gloves, too, may be vital pieces of equipment in the cold, for freezing hands will be unable to manipulate fastenings on clothing or hold map and compass satisfactorily.

Calf-length breeches worn with long socks give more freedom to leg movement than trousers which tend to create resistance; furthermore, with socks rolled down, ventilation is pleasantly increased. Alternatively, manufacturers such as Rohan and Mountain Equipment market strong but lightweight slacks with windproof/water-resistant properties and these have become fashionable and popular in recent years. For low level or short walks, especially in the White Peak, ordinary trousers would be quite adequate. Once you have become accustomed to exposing your legs, shorts are enjoyable to wear but, except in warm, settled weather, some extra leg covering should be carried.

Even in the hills, heat can pose a serious problem for walkers. I have known the Kinder plateau so dry you could wander at will over the normally boot-sucking hags and groughs, but you ended the day grimy with wind-blown peat dust. When the sun is high, protection for your head and shoulders is paramount and a good suncream will prevent burning. Fluid requirements will also be greatly increased and incidentally, every effort should be made to guard against inadvertently starting a fire in such conditions.

Heat exhaustion (hyperthermia) is not as uncommon in Britain as might be imagined, though exposure from the cold (hypothermia) is the greater threat. Hills in the Peak Park lie on comparable latitudes to Siberia and Labrador and, although our climate is moderated by the Atlantic Ocean, its potential for generating severe conditions should never be ignored, even in summer.

And so to footwear! With so much choice available these days, it is harder than it used to be to offer specific advice. In dry weather trainers will be fine for outings over easy terrain but will protect neither your ankles on uneven surfaces, nor your feet from being bruised by the stray falling stone. Sturdy leather shoes, though more robust, still lack ankle support. Heavy mountain boots, once the hallmark of 'real' walkers, have succumbed to the application of common sense which decrees that unless you need a high level of insulation from the cold—hand in hand perhaps, with the wearing of crampons—all that leather is totally unnecessary for ordinary hillwalking. I once did the Pennine Way in a pair of 'leather coffins' and can vouch for their energy-sapping, blister-inducing characteristics!

Plastic boots of one kind or another may hold a distinct advantage when bog-trotting in the Dark Peak, being impervious to liquid peat! I have never used them but I understand that for normal walking purposes they can be hot and none too comfortable.

It all boils down to horses for courses. Most walkers today favour a lightweight fell boot which cushions feet on stony ground, provides ankle support on steep slopes and gives a good degree of protection from rain, snow, and varieties of mud—from cattle manure to peat bog! Suitably waxed, most reputable makes will perform adequately and need no 'breaking in'. By the same token, however, there are limits to the water impermeability of leather and suede, so don't expect to keep dry feet all the time!

Gaiters or anklets that fit over the cuff and laces will add appreciably to a boot's effectiveness and are almost 'de rigeur' for expeditions over the peat plateaux where you can virtually guarantee the occasional 'boot in'. Elsewhere, they guard against thorny undergrowth and the ingress of small stones.

Great care is needed to prepare properly for winter expeditions over the high moors.

The vexed question of whether to wear one or more pairs of socks must be left to experience. I always wear two on the basis that at least some of the friction caused by walking is absorbed by the socks and not by my skin! But I know others who swear by a single pair. Either way, it is vital to wear your walking socks when trying on new boots, taking plenty of time to decide on the most comfortable model. Remember that feet spread when hot and subjected to repeated footfalls, so allow enough room to insert a finger down the heel and to waggle your toes.

Rucksacks and miscellaneous essentials conclude these thoughts on gear. On a summer jaunt through well inhabited countryside such as that found in parts of the White Peak, a small day-sack will accommodate all your needs. By contrast, winter expeditions over the northern moors require a much higher level of preparedness, reflected in more gear and a larger capacity sack. Backpackers carrying lightweight camping equipment use rucksacks with an internal or external frame to provide stability for the extra load.

The body soon chills when you stop walking, so it is always advisable to pack spare warm clothing. Other items not to be overlooked include emergency rations, adequate food and drink for the day, a small first-aid kit, telephone coins, toilet tissue, emergency whistle (and, in winter, a torch and survival bag), waterproofs, and map and compass (with the ability to use them!) It may not be your own misfortune that is alleviated by taking these precautions: I was once able to help a walker and his young daughter who had underestimated the length of their hike over Bleaklow. The little girl was seriously hungry (children have fewer reserves of energy to draw on) and my emergency supply of chocolate enabled her to continue and reach safety.

Safety in the hills is largely an attitude of mind. Sensible preparation and knowledge of your own capabilities will ensure that even in difficult conditions a walk is enjoyed and successfully concluded. In or near populated lowlands few objective risks are involved, but more ambitious hikes demand thoughtful planning if you are to avoid the risk of an ignominious retreat or—worse still—a Mountain Rescue call-out. Winter expeditions over the High Peak moors should always be taken seriously: your equipment and walking abilities can be sorely tested, and safety margins—particularly daylight hours—are considerably reduced.

Very occasionally, illness or injury will upset the best laid plans and it is at such times that decisive action will minimise delays in obtaining help. Utilising any available shelter, make the victim as comfortable and warm as possible, note down the 6-figure map reference for the incident's location and call the police by dialling 999 from the nearest phone: they will decide what procedures to set in motion. Peak Park Mountain Rescue teams are called out, on average, once a week—often as a result of people overestimating their competence or stamina.

In the event of an emergency, the International Distress Call should be used to help searchers locate your position. It is: 6 long signals per minute (eg. torch flashes or whistle blasts), answered by 3 such signals per minute.

It would be folly not to obtain an up-to-date weather forecast before embarking on more serious routes. British Telecom's 'Weathercall' service is more specific than general radio and television bulletins, and National Park Information Centres should also be able to help (See 'Useful Addresses'). There are many advantages to walking alone, but only if you are an experienced hillwalker: going in small groups significantly enhances the safety element, as will leaving a route-card containing details of your itinerary and expected return time with a responsible person. It is, naturally, important to inform them when you have completed the walk.

Walking conditions in the Peak District can vary enormously, from a wasteland of eroded peat around Bleaklow Head (top) to the sheltered beauty of Wolfscote Dale in limestone country (bottom).

About The Walks

Precisely what constitutes a 'classic' walk is open to discussion. It cannot hinge entirely on subjective experience, however, for one person's glorious day out becomes, under different circumstances, another person's miserable disappointment. From many dictionary definitions of 'classic', the most appropriate seems to be 'of lasting interest or significance'. In practice this has meant highlighting as many of the Peak Park's distinguishing characteristics as possible, each walk being endowed with a theme linking together noteworthy features. This is one of Europe's busiest National Parks and you will rarely tread where thousands have not trodden before you. This does not imply that the walks themselves are congested, only that established footpaths are followed for most of the time—sometimes a necessity when crossing Access Land or farmland. Concern is mounting over path erosion and the effects walkers have on moorland flora and fauna, so every effort should be made to minimise damage and to respect the Country Code.

I have tried to select walks that offer something for everyone: a few, therefore, are short and cross easy country—perfectly suitable for family outings or for the less mobile. At the other end of the scale, long-distance routes will challenge the fittest, requiring a high level of stamina and sound navigational skills. The majority of walks fall between these two extremes. Amounts of ascent and the degree to which you are exposed to the elements depend on location. Walks in the Dark Peak are generally more serious and possess less shelter, but tussles with the weather can occur anywhere and at any time, so the maxim should always be, go prepared!

Special mention should be made of the Peak Park's Ranger Service whose presence you may well encounter while out walking. Inaugurated in 1954 to patrol the then newly negotiated access areas, the Service now covers the entire National Park. Four District Rangers, a dozen Area Rangers and eight Seasonal Rangers are supplemented by around 170 part-timers and 200 volunteers. Conservation Volunteers also do sterling work by making repairs and improvements to this much visited landscape.

A Ranger's work includes such diverse activities as liaising with local people who live and work in the Park, offering assistance to visitors, helping livestock in difficulties, fighting moorland fires, and initiating mountain rescue.

Every attempt has been made to spread the following compilation of walks evenly from north to south, east to west, and to introduce readers to as many varied facets of the White

and Dark Peak regions as space allows. However, I make no claim that the selection represents all the possibilities for walks of quality in the Peak District—far from it! Inevitably, my choices are based on a personal preference for one route over another, and on fond recollections percolating through from a rich store of memories accumulated over many years. With intelligent use of map and compass, and reference to guidebooks (eg Mark Richards' excellent series published by Cicerone Press), any of the walks could be shortened, extended or joined up to meet individual needs. Indeed, the scope for improvising your own routes is virtually limitless once you have become acquainted with the region.

The walks are arranged in the book from south to north across the National Park, based on the latitude of their starting points. Each route is preceded by useful information but please note that approximate timings relate to an unhurried pace and take no account of halts for meals, photography, sightseeing, etc.

I have always found the 1″ Tourist Map of the Peak District ideal for locating and planning walks, and the two 1:25,000 Outdoor Leisure maps (White Peak and Dark Peak) indispensable for identifying detail. However, some walkers find the 1:50,000 OS Landranger sheets more manageable for general navigation purposes. (NB: Parts of the National Park area are omitted from the Outdoor Leisure maps, so check before setting out if you intend to rely on them).

I hope to have painted a balanced picture which newcomers to the Peak Park will find both informative and stimulating. Perhaps, too, walkers already familiar with this diverse and beautiful region will have happy memories rekindled and will be encouraged to rediscover old haunts.

Facing page: **Hazleton Clump.**

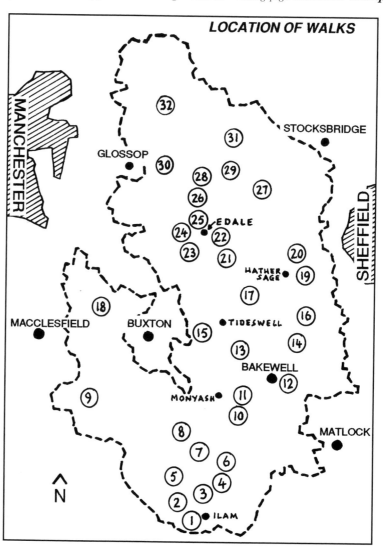

WALK 1: *Villages at the Southern Gateway*

Start/Finish: Blore Pastures car park. **Access:** By minor road north off the A52 about 5 miles (8km) west of Ashbourne. Nearest railway stations on the Matlock line. **Distance:** 4.5 miles (7.5km)—allow about 3 hours. **Terrain:** Undulating and often muddy field paths, farm tracks and country lanes. **Maps:** OS Landranger Sheet 119. Outdoor Leisure White Peak.

Left: **Ilam and the Manifold Valley from Bunster Hill.**

Facing page: **Ilam Church, below hills at the gateway to Dove Dale.**

Blore and Ilam are situated just inside the National Park boundary a few miles north-west of the market town of Ashbourne. They stand not only at the threshhold of the White Peak but in a very real sense of the Pennines too. Aside from the unacceptable erosion and congestion it would cause, a true Pennine Way would start, perhaps, at Ilam (where there is a large youth hostel) and thread its way north through limestone dales and uplands to the present terminus at Edale.

This may be a short walk, but Ilam, with its Alpine-style cottages and neo-Gothic Hall, acts as a focal point in a landscape of modest yet curiously dramatic hills. Unlike Dove Dale's sheer-sided gorge a stone's throw away to the east, the Manifold valley spreads itself around river meanders, showing signs of settlement and cultivation which date back many centuries.

It seems quite extraordinary that having risen close to each other on Axe Edge and having carved virtually parallel courses south to their confluence near Ilam, the rivers Dove and Manifold should present such different faces. In fact, as we shall see on the walk, the Manifold, far from entertaining visitors with babbling waters like the Dove, disappears shyly at Wettonmill. For 4 or 5 miles (6.5 to 8km) it follows a system of shakeholes, faults and caverns—a subterranean landscape rarely seen—to emerge at the Boil Hole in the grounds of Ilam Hall.

Only in rainy seasons will the Manifold behave like a conventional river, but then many of the White Peak dales are now dry. Limestone formed from the skeletons of tiny sea creatures (much as present-day coral reefs accumulate, but fossilised of course) is readily dissolved by rainwater. Water draining off the land is inclined to sink into underground hollows thus created instead of flowing along river beds, but if the water table is high this phenomenon is less evident.

Blore Pastures National Park car park, with its picnic enclosure and fine open views of Bunster Hill and Thorpe Cloud, makes a trouble-free base for this walk, though off-season you could park near Blore Church (with appropriate consideration for passing farm vehicles etc) or at Ilam Hall. Stiles guide you downhill over estate pastures and near Oxleisure Farm (surely a derivation from 'ox meadow' where plough teams once grazed?) you join the unfenced road over Ilam Bridge.

Confronting you in the centre of a road junction is a 30-ft (9m) cross erected by the Victorian shipping magnate Jesse Watts-Russell in memory of his first wife, Mary. The entire village was relocated and rebuilt by Londoner Watts-Russell, producing the kind of architectural extravagance you would scarcely expect in the Peak Park. Alpine-style cottages, tile-

hung and with boarded gables, are not only curiosities but are carefully tended, their flower-bedecked gardens contributing to Ilam's periodic 'Best Kept Village' aspirations.

Instead of walking through parkland along Ilam Hall's drive, turn left at Dovedale House on a pathway to Ilam Church. Despite some insensitive restoration in the mid-1800s, it is an ancient building and contains an interesting miscellany of features such as a Saxon font and the fine St. Bertram's Chapel. Ahead, a kissing gate leads out to Ilam Hall, a massively dour edifice with terraced gardens and a National Trust shop.

The original Hall, dating from 1546, was rebuilt in a battlemented and ostentatious neo-Gothic style by Jesse Watts-Russell as part of his 'grand vision' in the 1820s. Had it not been for the timely intervention of Sir Robert McDougall in 1934, when the Hall was in the process of being demolished, it might have vanished for good. As it transpires, the remaining portion was saved by Sir Robert who subsequently presented it to the National Trust. In summer, tea rooms at the back provide refreshment and the building now houses a youth hostel, always well patronised by field study groups in addition to passing hikers, cyclists and others.

You now either branch left down past a well to the erstwhile St. Bertram's Bridge, or simply descend steps to reach the Manifold's resurgence at Boil Hole. What follows is undoubtedly the easiest part of the walk—a stroll along Paradise Walk, passing the Battle Stone and Hamps Springs, another watercourse reappearing after a Stygian episode below ground! An alternative path descending from the Hall's gardens joins in for a half mile of riverside pleasure (even if the bed is dry), whereupon you reach River Lodge and possible payment of a toll (2p, I believe!) to cross the private garden.

Staying with the Throwley road as it swings left over green meadowland beside the Manifold brings you to Rushley Bridge and, a little farther on uphill, to Rushley Farm. Off the acute road bend, a track leads on to Musden Grange and if your boots have remained clean thus far, prepare for a muddying! A short way beyond the farmyard you fork left by a wall to ascend Abbot's Banks, hillsides flanking Musden Wood; higher up, a waymark will be seen where a direct path comes in from the Manifold footbridge passed on Paradise Walk.

You soon reach idyllically sited Upper Musden, a tree-sheltered farmstead overlook-

ing the Manifold valley which, alas, was too far off the beaten track to survive into our age of road access, electricity and telephones. Although many Pennine barns and farmhouses are enjoying a new lease of life as second homes or properties for commuters, a sad legacy of abandonment remains. The trend is, of course, nationwide and in my travels on foot to inaccessible or remote places I am often moved by the sight of homes—cherished and lived in for generations—ending their lives reduced to rubble by the unforgiving elements.

In and immediately out of the farmyard, you veer left over a stile and drop to a clear bridleway leading above Hinkley Wood. From numerous viewpoints the tree-crowned, circular hillock of Hazleton Clump insists on being noticed! There are many such prominences in the White Peak, useful landmarks for estimating your position, but in this instance public access to the summit is not available. Instead, you pass round its lower skirts to emerge on the Blore road by a fence stile.

For a speedy return to Blore Pastures car park, you could cut down left over old ridge-and-furrow pasture, short-cutting the road corner. But why not wander down to Blore, a sleepy hamlet south of the crossroads.

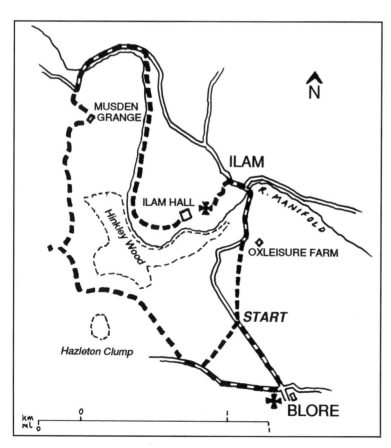

Above: **Ilam Hall.**

Facing page: **Beeston Tor and the River Manifold.**

WALK 2: *Grindon, Musden Wood and Beeston Tor*

Start/Finish: Grindon. **Access:** Reached by country road north of Waterhouses on the A52, 8 miles (13km) west of Ashbourne. Nearest railway stations—the Matlock line or Uttoxeter. **Distance:** 11 miles (17.5km)—allow 5 to 6 hours. **Terrain:** Consistently hilly. Tracks, rough paths and by-roads.
Maps: OS Landranger Sheet 119. Outdoor Leisure White Peak.

This is one of my favourite walks in the White Peak. Nowhere does it enter the arena of sightseeing, so paths tend to be free of people taking a stroll near cars and coaches. In that sense it is very much a walker's route, with several fairly steep and sustained (by White Peak standards) ascents.

Apart from the Manifold and Hamps rivers, none of the landmarks you encounter appear specially significant on a tourist map of the area, yet there are few routes to compare with this one for beauty and diversity: it is as if the walk's separate attributes—drystone walled fields, river valleys, deep woodland, rocky outcrops and the unsung delights of a quiet upland village—all combine to form a harmonious experience epitomising the delights of getting out and about in the Peakland landscape.

In essence you are making a loop round Throwley Moor—a wedge of high ground bounded to east and west by the Manifold and Hamps valleys and rising to 1145ft (349m) in the vicinity of Cart Low. Grindon itself, some

The walk begins at Grindon's cathedral-like parish church.

1037ft (316m) above sea level, lies to the west while Bincliff, visited towards the end of the walk, also approaches the magic 1000-ft (305m) contour. In between these elevated locations typical of the White Peak plateau are valleys 600ft (180m) or so lower: because you are crossing the grain of the land, ups and downs are to be expected.

As Staffordshire moorland villages go, Grindon ('Green Hill') seems quiet and unassuming. Set high above the Manifold and Hamps gorges and only modestly interested in attracting tourists, it nevertheless possesses two pubs—The Cavalier and The Red Lion—which will gladden the hearts of those who like to end (or start!) a walk with a tipple.

The cathedral-like parish church has no particular architectural merit, being wholly Victorian, but stands on a much older church site of Saxon origin. Its very prominent spire must, if nothing else, rate as an asset in identifying the village from afar. Inside you will find a memorial plaque to six R.A.F. men from the Gloucestershire base of Fairford who, along with two press photographers, died when their aircraft crashed on Grindon Moor in blizzard conditions during the severe winter of 1947. As the inscription informs us, the men had been '. . . bringing relief to the stricken villages . . .': Wetton, Grindon, Butterton and Onecote had been cut off by huge snowdrifts and food had had to be dropped by parachute.

The best car parking is to be found west of the churchyard and the walk sets off from the village's south-west corner, due south on a stony track flanked by fields. A beautiful June day here lodges in my memory. Fragrant breezes caressed ripening hay suffused with buttercups, and the air was alive with skylarks: it was one of those sparkling days when colours, smells and sounds seem more vivid that at any other time of year. In the valleys, sunlight filtered through foliage onto deep beds of nettles and cow parsley while insects hovered over damp hollows.

Soon the way loses height, zig-zags through Deepdale and passes through a farmyard before wending onwards with the sharp flank of Waterfall Low to your right. At a bend you fork off left over a stile and down past a barn usually surrounded by cattle. Stiles confirm this less well walked stretch which dips into woods and crosses the Hamps by a footbridge opposite Lee House.

Faulting in the limestone strata swallows the Hamps river just below Waterhouses, so don't be surprised if the bed is dry! Even though it clearly took a watercourse of prodigious volume to excavate the Hamps valley during the last Ice Age, today's vestigial river prefers to hide underground, rarely showing its full

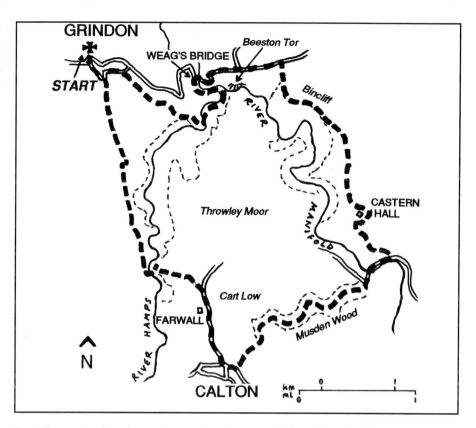

face. The surfaced track running north and south owes its existence to the Leek and Manifold Light Railway which folded in 1934 after only 30 years of service. Its trackbed was adopted by Staffordshire County Council as a public amenity for walkers and cyclists (see 'Four Railway Trails').

The climb up from Lee House into a minor side valley is quite unremitting and muddy in places. Towards the top you branch right over field stiles to join the B road which has swung round from Rushley Bridge, past Throwley Hall and up over Throwley Moor. This you now follow south for about 1200m mile to Calton, passing en route between the handsome farmstead of Farwall and the circular hill of Cart Low. It is unnecessary to enter Calton itself, so at the ensuing road junction keep left along Back Lane and in 300m look for a stile on the left. This will set you on a north-easterly course through sheep and cattle pasture fields, curving right into the sinuous upper reaches of Musden Wood.

Peaceful and enclosed, the habitat of Musden Wood contrasts pleasantly with open countryside, forming an interlude of special quality in the walk. Many of the characteristics we expect of woodland are present: bird species such as chaffinch and willow warbler—even woodpecker—as well as signs of shy animal activity. A wealth of wild flowers include the familiar white star clusters of ran-

soms (wild garlic) and drifts of bluebells in springtime.

Trees are spasmodic at first but become denser lower down. At my last visit I had to fight through undergrowth here and there, but it was summertime and efforts had been started to clear the thorn scrub. One of the problems with woodland paths is their vulnerability to this kind of obstruction if not used regularly by walkers and cleared by landowners. Fallen trees pose an even greater hazard and can effectively close down a public right of way for months before remedial action is taken.

After perhaps half an hour of rough going, you emerge from cattle-churned mud at Rushley Farm amongst chickens and ducks. The walk's next objective, Castern Hall, is set in a fold of hills above the opposite bank of the River Manifold. To reach it you cut back left on the Hall's access lane 400m beyond Rushley Bridge and walk uphill to confront the building itself—quite a grand façade considering its rather exposed position. The Hurt Family's occupation commenced in 1560 with Nicholas Hurt and its original estate land extended right over Ilam Tops to below Hurt's Wood in Hall Dale.

Passing round behind the Hall, your way lies along a gated track to the left, then up across strip lynchets of considerable antiquity. They certainly pre-date the big grange pastures which sweep up from the river with few dividing walls—once sheep runs managed by monks from Burton Abbey. Compared to this fertile reach of the Manifold valley, ancient settlements are conspicuous by their absence in neighbouring Dove Dale's cramped gorge.

Spoil from the Highfield Lead Mine on your right is quickly followed by a much more extensive area of waste and disused shafts at Bincliff. Mine adits pepper the wooded valley side and should act as a strong deterrent against wandering from the scarp-top path. Indeed, much of the Peak District is riddled with the remains of lead mining activity—mostly in the form of collapsed or capped shafts and the sparse ruins of stone sheds, or 'coes'.

Although the more productive mines were equipped with horse, water or steam-powered machinery, and some opencast workings created miniature gorges such as Dirtlow Rake near Castleton, the majority were very modest affairs. Typically, two or three owners working part time would extract about 10 tons of ore (galena, or lead sulphide) per year, veins often being of poor quality and size. Complex laws and customs surrounding the industry further limited enterprise and accidents were common, so a miner's life was undoubtedly hard. Speculation mounted to fever pitch during the nineteenth century, but already ore reserves were depleted. Although a few important strikes still occurred—notably Gang Mine at Cromford—a drastic decline in the market price of lead ore sounded the industry's death knell: with few exceptions, mining had ceased before the turn of the twentieth century.

Abandoned workings are almost invariably unsafe and should not be explored by the casual visitor. That's no hardship here, however, for the graceful curves of the River Manifold below (its bed at least, if no water is running!), backed by Cheshire Wood and Throwley Moor, will certainly steal the limelight.

Ahead, the ground falls gently to Larkstone Lane, part of a net of by-ways connecting Alstonefield, Hope and Wetton with Grindon and villages further west. You turn left with the descending tarmac which ends in convulsive zig-zags above Weag's Bridge. Here you will once again meet the Manifold Track, turning south along it to a car park and picnic site at the confluence of the rivers Hamps and Manifold below Beeston Tor.

Stepping stones west of Beeston Tor Farm are used by rock climbers to reach the base of this popular crag but are sometimes impassable when the Manifold is in spate. Non-climbers will be content with a 'worm's eye' view of this impressive buttress of reef limestone—the last such feature in the Manifold gorge which hereafter softens and opens out on its way to join the Dove east of Ilam. Hidden at the foot of Beeston Tor, St. Bertram's Cave yielded evidence of Iron Age and Romano-British occupation, along with a find of Saxon coins, when excavated earlier this century.

Resuming southerly progress along the line of the old railway beneath Soles Coppice and Oldpark Hill, you need to watch for a gate and stile on the right at an acute right-hand bend.

This doubles back then swings up into a side valley. On the climb back towards plateau level, you pass two substantial meres, after which field stiles lead you to a walled lane. At Porch Farm a left turn directs feet to The Cavalier which by now, having encountered no other hostelry on the entire outing, might seem more than usually tempting!

Facing page: **Thorpe Cloud stands sentinel over the entrance to Dove Dale.**

Below left: **Big grange pastures near Castern were once sheep runs managed by monks from Burton Abbey.**

Below right: **Looking back to Beeston Tor from the path below Grindon.**

WALK 3: *Dove Dale*

Start/Finish: Dove Dale car park. **Access:** North-west of Ashbourne, reached off the Thorpe to Ilam road. Nearest railway stations—Uttoxeter and the Matlock line. **Distance:** Route A—3 miles (5km) (one way); Route B—8½ miles (13.5km). Allow about 2 hours and 5 hours respectively. **Terrain:** Route A—a flat, broad, valley bottom pathway. Route B—rugged and often narrow paths with numerous ups and downs. **Maps:** OS Landranger Sheet 119. Outdoor Leisure White Peak.

'Was you ever in Dovedale? I assure you there are things in Derbyshire as noble as in Greece or Switzerland.' So wrote Lord Byron in the early years of the nineteenth century. Today Dove Dale—honeypot of the Peak District—has become a mecca for trippers and strollers who, with minimal effort, can gaze upon the wonders of one of Britain's best known natural tourist attractions.

This is not to denigrate the scenery or the valley walk to Milldale, for the limestone gorge is every bit as enthralling as it is cracked up to be! However, in recent years there have been changes. With considerable courage, the National Trust has cleared a good deal of ash woodland and scrub that hitherto had threatened to obscure many of the famous rock features. The valley path, too, was widened and consolidated to withstand the footfalls of countless thousands of visitors, so newcomers should not expect a wild, untrammelled trail.

A book of classic walks in the Peak District could hardly turn its back on Dove Dale, even though the beauty spot needs no extra publicity. I therefore offer two menus for exploration: Route A takes you past all the 'sights' from Thorpe Cloud to Milldale and apart from a short climb at Lover's Leap entails no gradients worth mentioning—an ideal outing for the less active. Some private transport arrangement to pick you up at Milldale would remove the necessity of retracting your steps; alternatively you could return along one of the higher level (though more strenuous) paths covered by Route B.

Route B has sporting aspirations! Eschewing the dale bottom for a circuit just above the precipitous enclosing hillsides, it is designed for those who enjoy ups and downs and don't mind sometimes narrow paths over rough, steep terrain. Flexibility is built in, since either outward or return legs could resort to the valley pathway.

The River Dove emerges from its cliff-girt course beneath the thrust of Bunster Hill, swinging south-westwards in a tight bend before flowing out through green fields to join the Manifold. A large car park has been established in a river loop near Thorpe Cloud and forms an obvious base from which to set out on either of the routes described below. Refreshments are available during the holiday season.

Route A: The Dove Dale Gorge

Glacial meltwater from the last Ice Age scoured out the extraordinary ravine about to be explored, the present River Dove being a mere shadow of its former self. Nevertheless,

in spate it will prevent a crossing of the stepping stones adjacent to Lin Dale, so check the river level before walking along the west bank: if high, cross the footbridge to the east bank path along the base of Thorpe Cloud's screes.

In summer, when the Dove often dries to a sluggish trickle, the square-cut stepping stones, installed by the Victorians who also christened several rock features in the gorge, will pose few problems. Their crossing is obligatory for athletes participating in the annual 'Dovedale Dash', a local fell-run, and I remember one occasion when the stones were completely submerged: there were several spectacular slips and everyone got very wet!

There can be no mistaking the way as you head upstream towards the deeply wooded fold of hills ahead. Towering crags on the opposite, Staffordshire, bank are Dovedale Castle Rocks. (Throughout its length from Axe Edge to the Trent, the Dove is county boundary between Staffordshire and Derbyshire). River weirs, another Victorian addition to the natural scene, were created to form fishing pools when river levels were low.

Lover's Leap headland has to be surmounted but the stepped climb is not hard and there are magnificent views of the Twelve Apostles, a family of rock towers which had been almost lost to view before woodland clearance. Descending, you pass Tissington Spires, impressive leaning pinnacles of reef limestone up to your right which have also benefited from the removal of invading ashwood. Jacob's Ladder, a lone buttress, rears skywards on the Staffordshire bank.

Biblical names for features in Dove Dale were almost certainly coined by early travel writers who, in the true spirit of nineteenth century Romanticism, tended to lace description with exaggeration and references to the 'good book' in order to invoke a response of awe—even terror—at the prospect of natural grandeur. It may all seem tame to us, inured as we are to images, even experience, of exotic places. Yet those early tourists saw everything afresh in an environment largely unsullied by man's attentions. Paths were sketchy, roads in rural areas non-existent, and many natural phenomena remained unexplained and mysterious. Could it be that modern rationalism which devalues intuitive or supernatural insights actually dulls our appreciation of the world around us?

Beyond the narrow indentation of Sharplow Dale, you come to the Natural Arch and a chance to scramble up to Reynard's Cave. Looking back, the Dove appears framed by the arch while high on the skyline above Dovedale Wood stands Air Cottage.

So precipitous are the crags at The Straits

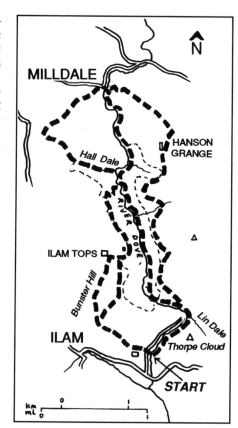

that an artificial duckboard path has had to be laid for safe pedestrian passage. A little further along you pass beneath Lion's Head Rock and into the heart of Dove Dale by Pickering Tor, with Ilam Rock's elegant blade soaring just across the footbridge. One of the Dove's great charms is its relative inaccessibility to motor traffic, so although there may be no shortage of fellow humans on the various trails that border it—at least in its more popular reaches—we are all spared the noise and fumes that roads invariably bring.

Curving east past Hall Dale (ascended on Route B), you suddenly confront Dove Holes, two sizeable caves formed by the original glacial torrent, though of disappointingly shallow depth. Technically the more open valley beyond the junction with Nabs Dale is no longer Dove Dale, but there is no deterioration in the scenery. Although you could turn for home at Dove Holes and enjoy the 2 miles (3km) of outstanding beauty all over again (walking in the opposite direction invariably changes your perception of the landscape), many will press on to Milldale, either to pick up a lift or to take refreshment in the popular little cafe there.

Raven's Tor is the last rocky eminence of real consequence, whereafter you follow the Dove's meanders opposite small walled fields where easier slopes have allowed pasture to develop. Crossing Viator's Bridge, a relic from the days of packhorse trains, brings you to Milldale hamlet, squeezed picturesquely alongside the river at the junction with Hope Dale. A car park has been opened just up the Hope road which leads, via Stanshope, back to Ilam and thence to the Dove Dale car park.

Route B: Hilltops and Woods Above Dove Dale

A good deal of legwork is involved in this circular amble round the upper edge of Dove Dale and its tributary valleys. Uninterrupted rights of way do not exist above all the dale-sides, so in a few places the walk is forced down into Dove Dale and back out again, increasing the expenditure of energy but also adding to one's appreciation of this unique environment. It is one of my favourite walks, especially out of season, and is guaranteed to work up a hearty appetite.

Unexpectedly, perhaps, you begin by walking away from high ground at the gates of Dove Dale, striking off west instead over stiles and fields towards Ilam. At the Izaac Walton Hotel you branch right across pasture, heading for a 'col' or saddle in the rising skyline of Bunster Hill. A steepening rocky path gets you there and opens up marvellous views south over Ilam and the Manifold valley.

You can cross the col, follow the contouring path north and climb by a wall to Ilam Tops, or you can attack the Bunster Hill ridge direct. It is a stiff climb but an exhilarating one, ending at a cluster of tumuli and leading via stiles, a mere and a barn to Ilamtops Farm. At the road gate you turn right on a surfaced track to Air Cottage, set high above crags and woods around Jacob's Ladder and Tissington Spires.

Gates lead round to a track and ladder stile, from where you traverse the top edge of Dovedale Wood before plunging down steep zig-zags through Hurt's Wood—a recently made and well graded path replacing that depicted on O.S. maps which had become a muddy scramble. A short distance downstream stand Ilam Rock and Pickering Tor, well worth detouring to for arguably this is Dove Dale's 'inner sanctum', strictly reserved for those who take the trouble to arrive on foot.

This foray to the valley bottom is due to there being no footpath above Hurt's Wood, but an ascent of secluded Hall Dale is ample compensation. One winter's morning in this dry, cragbound side valley, my companion and I trod deep, virgin snow, shadowing the spoor of badger and fox and marvelling at the utter tranquillity so close to the gregarious parade of walkers in Dove Dale itself.

At the dale head you cross a stile on the

right and climb to Stanshope Pasture Lane, branching left off it on a downhill course through field stiles to the Hope road and Milldale. Perfectly positioned at the halfway mark, the little cafe will satisfy any hunger or thirst and will provide a pleasant indoor interlude unless the day is warm and a seat outside is preferred.

Thus fortified, a new start is made by crossing Viator's Bridge and climbing the old zig-zag way up to Hanson Toot ('toot' meaning 'lookout', which describes perfectly this eyrie above Milldale) Trending right, you now mount successive pasture fields with intriguing retrospective views over the sinuous windings

Near Hanson Grange Farm, high above Dove Dale.

of hills flanking Beresford Dale. You veer right at a mere to pass above Hanson Grange Farm before dropping from a gate into the rocky defile of Nabs Dale. Although for the last time, once again the absence of a suitable high-level path obliges the way to lose all the height just gained—you were warned!

Immediately past Dove Holes, an old path slants left through Upper Taylor's Wood to the top of diminutive Pickering Dale, now high above its unseen Tor. Descending alongside a wall, you pass through a minor re-entrant valley and contour along undulating hillside. Several opportunities to peer over the precipitous lip of Dove Dale present themselves, but one must counsel caution for not everywhere could a fall be checked.

Shaplow Dale bites deep into the main valley, taking the path back with it. Soon you have aerial views down over Tissington Spires and across to the outward leg of the walk, skirting an area of gorsy scrub through another shallow dry valley. Having crossed the ridge above Lover's Leap, you may find the path line peters out temporarily in the dense turf, but despite steepish ground it soon reasserts itself and with a final dog-leg bend deposits you on the valley track not far from the stepping stones.

There is absolutely no reason why the walk should not terminate here with a gentle stroll back to the car park. However, it will not have escaped your attention that one hill remains unscaled—Thorpe Cloud. If you've puff enough for 500ft (152m) of ascent, your efforts will be richly rewarded since the summit stands sentinel-like over the entrance to Dove Dale and represents a transition from lowland to hill country when approached from any southerly point.

A well-worn path strikes uncompromisingly up the north ridge, as challenging and strenuous as any on a 'real' mountain! But at 942ft (287m) above sea level Thorpe Cloud is only a mountain in miniature so that almost before you expect it the rocky crest is upon you and there is nowhere to go but down. Few viewpoints provide finer displays of the local topography and, though endearingly modest in stature, your perch is endowed with a certain spice from a hint of exposure. The grassy west flank offers a straightforward descent and leads out, via a short rocky postscript, to the footbridge just along from the Dove Dale car park.

Walkers congregate at the bottom of Lin Dale to watch competitors in the Dovedale Dash cross the river stepping stones.

Once out of its gorge, the River Dove meanders through green fields—a view south-east from the summit of Thorpe Cloud.

Facing page: **Lees Barn (centre) on the country road to Biggin, seen from the Tissington Trail.**

WALK 4: *Parwich, The Tissington Trail and Eaton Dale*

Start/Finish: Parwich. **Access:** Parwich lies west of Wirksworth, between the B5056 and A515. Nearest railway station—Whatstandwell. **Distance:** 8½ miles (14km). **Terrain:** Field paths and tracks and a disused railway trackbed. **Maps:** OS Landranger Sheet 119. Outdoor Leisure White Peak.

Near the south-eastern boundary of the National Park, not far from the market town of Ashbourne, limestone uplands fall towards the confluence of Bletch, Havenhill Dale and Bradbourne brooks. On the edge of this rising swell of land sits the pretty, stone-built village of Parwich.

Parwich church is mainly Victorian and, around it, hilly streets connect parts of the village which seem rather spread about. But it is Parwich Hall which totally dominates. Built of brick in the mid eighteenth century against steepening hillside, it strikes an incongruous note in an otherwise architecturally harmonious setting; this drawing attention to itself was, of course, deliberate and endows the Hall with a certain intrinsic interest.

This walk sets out to explore a wedge of land to the east of Dove Dale. Once you have attained the 1000-ft (305m) contour, there are relatively few gradients to contend with and views are excitingly wide-ranging. You begin from the top of the village just east of the hospital where a path strikes up over often slippery slopes through scrubby woodland—the only appreciable scramble on the whole route—to reach the plateau near Parwich Hill. Here, cloud shadows chasing across pale fields

held in a matrix of drystone walls paint landscapes typical of the high White Peak.

In wintertime you will encounter sheep and, perhaps, the occasional group of walkers who, like you, are attempting to locate the wall stiles linking together to form footpaths. Under snow conditions, particularly should your boots be first to mark the virgin crust, these stiles and careful navigation will constitute your passport to a successful walk. No-one condones scaling drystone walls except in an emergency, for they are often formidably high and it is almost impossible not to dislodge a stone or two in passing—damage for which the farmer has to count the cost.

By proceeding due north over gently rising ground you will soon cross a by-road near Hilltop Farm. A continuation of the field path almost directly opposite leads you over a broad shoulder of land then, unexpectedly, takes you down a steep slope to Lowmoor Farm. Perhaps my passing here has always been preceded by rain, but impressions of Lowmoor Farm are of mud, mud and more mud! It is set in a hollow where old quarry workings have filled with water; add to this copious quantities of cattle manure and you have a recipe for squelchy underfoot conditions!

Still virtually due north, the path penetrates narrow Lowmoor Plantation and passes a ruin. To your right the horizon lifts to Roystone Rocks, obscuring Roystone Grange around which a fascinating Archaeological Trail has been set up; it incorporates the remains of a medieval farm, traces of Roman occupation and evidence of ancient quarrying and mining (see Walk 6).

The cost of maintaining stone walls in good repair on these exposed hilltops is very considerable and, regrettably, it cannot always be met. At my last visit, old field boundaries north of Lowmoor Farm had fallen into dereliction, broken over the years by sheep, cattle, wind and weather. In fact, if the land is used simply for grazing, this neglect may be of little consequence, even if the visual effect is forlorn.

And so you wend your way through wall gaps and stiles to a farm lane west of The Nook with its conspicuous shelter belt of trees. This lane is now followed north-west for over 1½ miles (2.75km), climbing a little at first before levelling off and finally dropping to the main A515 road near Newhaven. There are views north to Aleck Low (1290ft—393m), one of the rounded, tree-topped prominences which characterise this part of the Peak Dis-

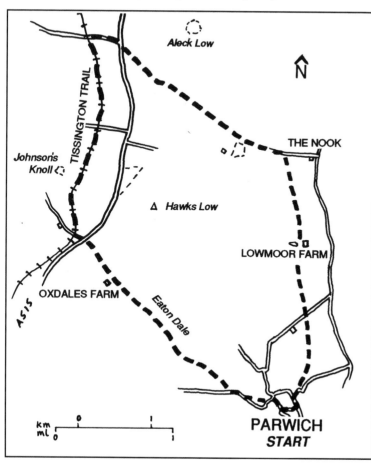

Sunshine breaks through morning mist beside the Tissington Trail.

trict, providing landmarks against which a compass bearing may be checked and progress measured.

After walking along the A515 for 100m to the right, you turn left towards Biggin and in 400m left again up onto the trackbed of the old Ashbourne to Buxton railway. Adopted as the Tissington Trail for leisure use by the general public, its gentle curves and lack of gradients offer the easiest walking, although in my experience you can risk various forms of foot discomfort by pushing your pace too hard on the unyielding surface!

Freed for the present from the need to navigate over farmland, you have time a-plenty to admire the beauty of this largely man-made landscape. At around 1250ft (380m) above sea level, it is comparable in altitude to many parts of the Dark Peak, yet there the similarity ends. Intricate field patterns superimposed upon the green and white of limestone country, the intimacy of dale and brook and a skyline punctuated by barns or clumps of trees all combine to contrast with the bolder sweep of less hospitable moors to the north. Having made such a comparison, it is also true that in hard winter conditions the White Peak loses its picturesque benevolence and that then, life for the farming community in particular can be severely affected.

By embankment and cutting the Tissington Trail swings south over a minor road near Bigginmoor Farm, passes Johnson's Knoll (another conspicuous copse-crowned hill) and crosses the Biggin/Hartington road near Lees Barn, a pleasing cluster of farm buildings in an almost archetypical pastoral setting. Here you must descend from the Trail through a wicket gate, walk beneath the bridge and cross the A515. A short way to the left on the other side you will find an old entrance gate to a disused lime quarry. Ahead, down a bank of old clinker spoil, you pick up the first in a sequence of squeeze stiles threading through narrow fields to pass Oxdales Farm. Views back to hills bordering the upper Dove are well worth savouring.

Imperceptibly at first, the ground falls downhill into Eaton Dale. One midwinter's day we found several rabbit and sheep skulls in the broad basin beyond Eatondale Wood. It is a strangely secluded place, frequented by few

Parwich—mid winter.

walkers and hemmed in lower down by a narrowing of the dale. In this sheltered hollow are a couple of meres and signs of medieval strip lynchets, but if a farmstead once existed here all remains of it have long since disappeared.

In the vicinity of a ruined barn there is a transition from upland pasture on limestone to ridge-and-furrow on heavy clay. The ensuing fields are negotiated corner to corner over land that, in times past, was almost certainly under intensive cultivation—witness the substantial plough-made ridges; today it is used to graze cattle.

Having crossed Middlehill Farm's access lane and dropped to Flaxdale Holding, it is but a short stride by minor road to Parwich. A more appropriate ending to the walk, however, branches left at a stile signed 'Lenscliff' and joins up five further stiles in quick succession, emerging close to Parwich Primary School at the western edge of the village.

WALK 5: *Thor's Cave, The Manifold Valley and Ecton Copper Mines*

Start/Finish: Wetton car park. **Access:** By country road south from Hulme End on the B5054, or west from the A515 via Alstonefield. Nearest railway station—Matlock. **Distance:** 10 miles (16km)—allow about 5 hours. **Terrain:** A combination of hilly and potentially muddy paths, level track, country lanes and one pathless section. Several stiff ascents. **Maps:** OS Landranger Sheet 119. Outdoor Leisure White Peak.

The serpentine meanders of the River Manifold, broad and uninhibited, contrast sharply with the Dove's cramped passage through steep-sided dales a few miles to the east. Because its valley floor is appreciably wider, there was even space beside the Manifold for a light railway (of which more later)—converted to a surfaced track in 1935 and widely appreciated by the walking fraternity. It is of particular value to anyone wishing to avoid gradients, awkward ground or obstructions.

This walk hinges on a block of elevated ground between the Dove and Manifold rivers, with the sleepy, grey-stoned village of Wetton as its base. Refreshments are available here during the summer at Manor House Farm and throughout the year at Ye Olde Royal Oak. In wintertime, food and drink is less easy to come by generally in the White Peak, since cafes such as that at Wetton Mill tend to close—if not permanently then weekdays at least.

If you walk south from Wetton's National Park car park for a few metres and turn right to the end of Wetton Street, you will see a 'Concessionary Path to Thor's Cave' forking left off the descending Wetton Mill road. Further down, the path bifurcates, the right fork dropping through woods to the Manifold valley; however, our immediate objective being Thor's Cave, it is best to fork left on the (waymarked) higher path. This undulates round and ends on the crag's summit—a recommended prelude to exploring the cave itself, though not perhaps in very wet or windy weather as there are sheer rock faces below to the north and west. In any case, it is necessary to descend by the same path for access to Thor's Cave, named after the Norse Thunder God and set 250ft (76m) above the valley.

Wetton churchyard contains the tomb of Samuel Carrington, village schoolmaster who, in collaboration with Thomas Bateman of Middleton-by-Youlgreave, unearthed evidence in 1864 of Thor's Cave having been occupied by man from the Stone Age to Romano-British times. The earliest of these visitors would have arrived in the Peak District at the end of the Great Ice Age, living in temporary rock shelters and caves such as this, where they left flint artefacts and bones from animals they had hunted. Other finds of later date included fragments of pottery, bronze brooches and iron knife-blades, but a good deal may have been lost by the relative carelessness of those first archaeological excavators.

Facing page: **Wetton Mill on the banks of the River Manifold.**

Slanting reef limestone forms the cave's floor—a lethally greasy surface when wet—and there is an inspiring view out through the great 30-ft (9m) vaulted entrance across the wooded Manifold valley to Ossoms Hill and beyond. To appreciate how this and other caves in a once extensive subterranean system were formed, it is necessary to visualise a land dominated by the action of ice and glacial meltwater during the many phases of the last Ice Age: the force and persistence of water flows needed to erode such features is almost unimaginable.

There are various smaller caves outside above the West Window—Thor's Fissure, Seven Ways and Elderbush, all of which have revealed signs of early man— but they are not readily accessible to visitors. Instead, you may choose to sit on a ledge of ground and contemplate the Manifold's picturesque northward course, with Wetton Hill to the right, or straightaway descend the stepped path to the river footbridge.

'River' may be a misnomer if it is summertime and you are confronted by a bed of stones! Underground, a system of passages, faults and caverns within the reef limestone accommodates the Manifold's normal flow between Wetton Mill Swallet and Boil Hole near Ilam Hall: only in times of heavy, prolonged rainfall when the water table rises will the Manifold gurgle and splash like a proper river should over this section.

Free from mud and steepnesses, you can now stride north on the Manifold Track. Scenery to left and right is of outstanding quality, a similar mix of luxuriant woodland and limestone outcrops to that found in Dove Dale, but here expanded with pasture and a sense of spaciousness. The Leek and Manifold Light Railway, a private, narrow-gauge (2ft 6in) enterprise, took 2 years to build and opened in 1904—what a delightful train ride it must have been! Its principal function was that of a milk train, with the main line connection at Waterhouses from 1919, but it was also intended to enhance the effectiveness of Ecton's copper mines west of Hartington and to serve the travelling needs of local communities. Unfortunately the dairy closed in 1933 and the line's other missions proved unprofitable so, only 30 years after its inception, it ceased operation in 1934. With commendable vision, Staffordshire County Council quickly adopted the 8 miles (13km) of trackbed between Hulme End and Waterhouses as a bridleway, laying a tarmac surface and opening up what has undoubtedly become a major public amenity in the National Park.

I have often reflected upon how a railway line could have been pushed through this beautiful dale in the first place. But today we take environmental matters seriously and perhaps it should be borne in mind that the era of widespread motor transport—public and private—was late arriving in rural areas where roads were poor or non-existent. In theory the railway should have flourished, but country folk rarely travelled far from home and despite the introduction of excursions at weekends and public holidays, passenger traffic was always thin. Had the line connected destinations of greater consequence the story might have ended differently.

However, it is an ill wind and failure was transformed to success from the point of view of public enjoyment of this delectable landscape. Walkers and cyclists have 4 railway trackbed options affording easy access to the White Peak, namely the Manifold, Tissington, High Peak and Monsal trails.

Within 20 minutes you will have arrived at Wetton Mill, a popular watering hole during the summer months when the cafe is open and you can sit outside with a drink and watch the world go by. Wetton Mill (now a farm) dates back to 1577, possibly earlier, and ground corn for three centuries. Today the complex of buildings belongs to the National Trust who have provided a car park just across the bridge.

Depending on the level of the water table, you can watch the River Manifold sink underground here (or further downstream) on its furtive, unseen journey to the grounds of Ilam Hall, deceiving those who take their OS maps too literally! Directly above the cafe, and easily reached, stands a limestone knoll peppered with interesting cavities, the largest of which—Nan Tor Cave—was found to have been used by Mesolithic man over 8000 years ago.

If the idea appeals, you could continue walking along the Manifold Track, picking up the route description at Ecton. However, with some climbing now in prospect, the main itinerary heads up the lane to Dale Head Farm, ducks beneath an overhead vacuum line (5ft 8in!) and rises over pasture in an intimate side dale. The Sugarloaf, a defiant bastion of reef limestone, is skirted to the left, whereafter you follow field stiles up into the broadening dale head. Meeting a bend in the lane from Broad Ecton Farm, you turn left through a gate towards Summerhill Farm but just before getting there veer off right towards the top of a shelter belt on Ecton Hill. As fate sometimes decrees, I have yet to visit this high ground in clement weather, my last foray on a May Day weekend having been lashed by heavy showers and a bitter wind.

Continuing ahead, you pass through a wall gap, then a narrow stile and in a few downhill metres turn right on a path contouring

Thor's Cave. Archaeological finds indicate occupation by man following the Great Ice Age.

high above the Manifold valley. Views, already good, extend even further once you have rounded a jutting corner of hillside. Ahead, a distinctive horseshoe of conifers surrounds spoil from the Dutchman copper mine, soon to be encountered at close quarters, while below it stands Radcliffe's Folly, its copper spire as conspicuous an architectural feature as any in the entire National Park! On closer inspection the building—unconnected with the copper mines which surround it and put up by one Arthur Radcliffe in the 1930s—appears to be in a sad state of repair and must present its existing occupant with all manner of structural problems.

Soon the path descends gently across a great concave basin of hillside. You ignore all trods to the left, finally reaching old walls and rubble—the remains of a smithy, carpenter's shop and engine house at Dutchman Mine. Farther on and a little higher stands the erstwhile engine house for Deep Ecton Mine, now used as a barn but once containing a Boulton and Watt steam engine employed to raise waste rock to the surface and to pump out water. Large quantities of spoil which once blighted these slopes were removed for use as railway ballast and in road building, restoring the valley more or less to its pre-mining state.

Ecton's copper-bearing ore, along with associated deposits of zinc and lead, brought great wealth to the Dukes of Devonshire and the Burgoynes of Bedfordshire who jointly owned the workings during the mines' heyday in the late eighteenth century. Deep Ecton Mine alone netted over £1,000,000—in those days a huge fortune—much of which went into the building of Chatsworth House and the development of Buxton as a spa town. Three hundred men, women and children were involved in removing the ore and crushing it above ground prior to its being transported out on pack mules to a smelting works at Whiston.

As its name suggests, Deep Ecton penetrated far underground and by the mid-1800s had reached a depth of 1380ft (420m), then the deepest mine in Britain. (Its open top still presents a hazard to the over-curious). Before the twentieth century had turned, Ecton's copper mines had already stopped production, the remaining ore having become too costly to extract and water having posed severe technical difficulties.

From the barn, a direct path drops steeply to a lower one leading into the lane past Radcliffe's Folly. Down at Dale Bridge you turn right along the Manifold Track through water meadows for about 1200m to arrive at Hulme End, the former railway terminus. Here, where the Dove and Manifold flow within a mile of each other, are car park, telephone, shop, campsite and a nearby pub.

The onward route first heads east for Hartington then south towards Alstonefield before branching left on a minor road for Beresford Dale. This interlude of little-used country lanes, in the absence of suitable footpaths, leads you east via Beresford Lane and Barracks farms to the footbridge at Beaver Ford. This is a lovely spot where the Dove weaves through meadows before entering the deep confines of Wolfescote Dale on its journey to celebrated Dove Dale. However, 100m before the road ends, a track on the right, punctuated by gates, leads along the base of Gratton Hill and through a rocky passage into the pastoral landscape of Narrowdale.

Ignored by many visitors to the area who flock to see Dove Dale and its environs, Narrowdale seems shy, almost secretive—an upland dalescape caught between the heights of Gratton and Narrowdale hills. Drystone walls dip gracefully with the curve of valley and hillside and there are good views back to Sheen Hill. You pass an abandoned Lister water pump which has been there for donkey's years and thread your way up through field enclosures, climbing a couple of permanently fastened gates and following the bridleway, right, to the Alstonefield road. This walk shuns Alstonefield village, though refreshments can be found (shop-cum-cafe and The George

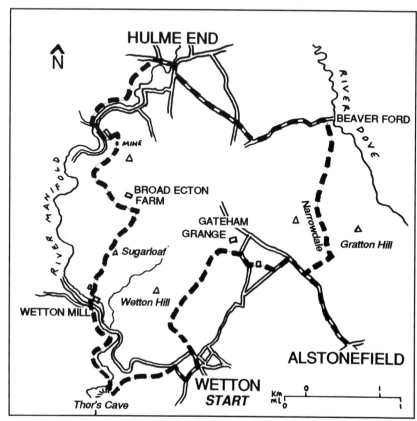

pub), or a pleasant half-hour spent admiring the church and a number of interesting buildings.

The shortest route back to Wetton strikes west across the head of Hope Dale, but I have concluded the expedition with a circuitous loop to take in what I consider to be a superb little hilltop north-east of Wetton. Reaching it involves a short walk along the Hulme End road, a left turn at the next junction and picking up a footpath on the right through Gateham Farm. At the lane ahead you turn right and take a path left off the bend, bringing you to the foot of steep hillside.

While paths diverge to left and right (both would lead you to Wetton), neither attains high ground so I recommend a direct ascent: it will certainly exercise legs and lungs but the height gain is only a modest 233ft (71m) and you are soon perched on the tumuli-crowned summit with a bird's-eye panorama spread out before you. This particular top is un-named on OS maps but I once christened it Gateham Hill in deference to Gateham Grange and Gateham Farm below.

Now heading for Wetton, you will discover a shallow saddle between this and another—slightly lower—top to the south-west. The depression is occupied by walled enclosures and I suggest you keep outside the right-hand (north-west) boundary. This line will give you excellent views of Wetton Hill, opposite, as well as a distant horizon formed by the western moors.

Eventually the ridge falls gently to a covered reservoir at the top of a track which will take you down to Manor House Farm. To regain the car park you continue straight ahead, turning right at the bottom end of the village.

Above: **The engine-house (now a barn) at Deep Ecton Copper Mine once held a Boulton & Watt steam engine used to raise spoil to the surface and to pump out water.**

Right: **From Wetton Hill there are views to the western moors.**

WALK 6: *The Roystone Grange Archaeological Trail*

Start/Finish: Minninglow car park. **Access:** ½ mile south of Pikehall on the A5012 between Cromford and Newhaven. Nearest railway station—Matlock. **Distance:** 5½ miles (9km)—allow 3 to 4 hours. **Terrain:** A railway trackbed trail, green lanes, country roads and field paths. Gentle gradients but muddy in places. **Maps:** OS Landranger Sheet 119. Outdoor Leisure White Peak.

So often in these crowded islands of ours, layers of evidence substantiating what we believe to be historical fact are lost to the plough or buried beneath roads and new building development. Sometimes in hilly regions, however, where past settlement reached its upper limits and where twentieth century man finds it uneconomic to exploit the land, signs of our ancestry remain intact. One such location lies here in the heart of the White Peak—somewhat off the tourist track but a classic walk of its kind, full of historical treasures.

Two factors lend distinction to this itinerary. First, the concurrence within a remarkably compact area of relics from fourth century Romano-British settlement, a monastic grange and drove roads from medieval times, and the more obvious manifestations of nineteenth century industrial activity. Second, this historical pot-pourri is set amidst all the distinctive features for which Derbyshire's limestone country is renowned and which become familiar to walkers who get out and about.

Minninglow car park is one of several established at strategic points along the High Peak Trail; equipped as picnic areas too, they offer ideal starting points for walkers, cyclists and horse-riders. With no refreshment places in prospect on this walk, however, it would be as well to bring your own food and drink; the nearest pub is the Sycamore at Parwich, some distance away by road.

You set off east over a minor road and along the cinder trackbed of the former Cromford and Highpeak Railway, originally conceived as a waterway to link the Cromford Canal with the Peak Forest Canal at Whaley Bridge (hence stations called 'wharves'). For technical and economic reasons it began life in 1830 as a railway line—one of the earliest operations in Britain.

At first, passenger coaches and freight waggons were hauled along by horses—later by locomotives—while stationary steam engines powered a cable system to winch waggons up the steeper inclines. Over the years, the fortunes of trackside quarries (the line's raison d'être) declined and with them the railway's usefulness. By 1967 the final working section between Friden and Parsley Hay had closed down. Four years later, $17\frac{1}{2}$ miles (28km) of track was adopted as a trail for use by the general public—a highly successful venture. Many trackside features and relics are still in situ, while throughout its length travellers are

presented with some of the finest White Peak landscape scenery.

Almost before you have started there are magnificent views south-east to the skyline hump of Minninglow. The high masonry embankment upon which you are walking does not become visible until you have gone beyond a curve in the trackbed; looking back, it takes on all the massive architectural qualities of a dam.

Reaching a quarry cutting, you will come across the rust-brown hulk of an old Smiths Rodley crane, once used to load stone onto waiting railway trucks. Here the trackbed swings south and crosses another substantial embankment, passing the collapsed beehive shape of a lime kiln and taking you to the junction with Minninglow Lane.

Just over to your right, half hidden behind overgrown grass and piles of rubble, stands the ruined base of a nineteenth century brick kiln. High-firing refractory bricks for use in steel industry furnace linings were produced here, employing deposits of silica sand extracted down near Minninglow Grange. Other sites for this process existed at Friden Grange and Harborough, both about 4 miles (6km) in either direction along the line; Minninglow's kiln, however, was the first to become operational.

You now leave the High Peak Trail through a gate on the left. Entering Gallowlow Lane, the customary yellow arrow waymarks are overpainted with black 'R's (denoting the

Roystone Archaeological Trail). Its name chillingly derived from 'hill surmounted by gallows', this ancient walled drovers' road traverses the White Peak plateau from Wirksworth to Hartington. For long stretches it retains its original form, though it changes name here and there. Minninglow itself forms a visual, if distant, focus for much of the walk. Now close at hand, you can make out its Neolithic chambered burial mound beneath a stand of sorry-looking, wind battered beech trees at 1220ft (372m) above sea level. Grazed by sheep, its flanks are scattered with stones but as there is no public access, exploration is regrettably not possible.

Gallowlow Lane dips then rises, and a stile on the right in a manifestly old wall leads you downhill past a mere and under an arch in the stone-built railway embankment. Stiles connect onwards; weighty stones at the base of the wall which accompanies you on the descent may well have been placed there during Roman times and subsequently built upon to define developing field boundaries through the ages. Crossing a paddock at the bottom of the hill, you reach a handgate onto the valley track just below Roystone Grange farm.

I now recommend a detour downdale to the chapel-like building standing alone next to some sheep pens. It was constructed at the beginning of this century to house a pump, cooled by water from a nearby spring, which sent air to primitive pneumatic drills used in

*Facing page: **Tree-covered Minninglow becomes a visual fulcrum for the walk.***

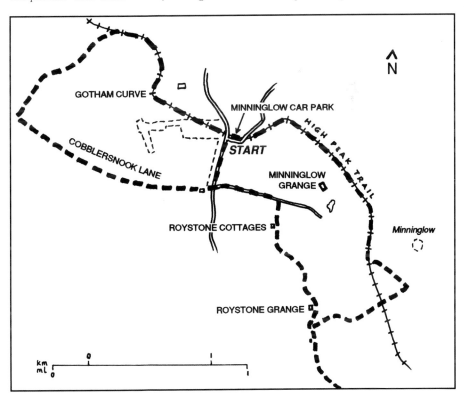

Facing page: **The chapel-like pumping house that once served adjacent hilltop quarries.**

Left: **The rusting hulk of a Smiths Rodley crane beside the High Peak railway trackbed.**

Below: **The present Royston Grange—a solid, eighteenth-century farmstead—stands on a much older site.**

quarries on the adjacent hilltops.

Of rather more significance are the excavated outlines of medieval grange buildings on a terrace below the dew pond facing you. During the reign of Henry II, the Cistercian Abbey of Garendon in Leicestershire was donated '. . . pasture, beasts and appurtenances in the vill of Revenstones . . .' (Roystone) by a local lord—Adam de Herthill. Poor grazing and rough moorland in Britain's northern reaches were considered to be of little value by the landowning gentry and were often made over as gifts to Abbey foundations who established outlying grange farms. Manned largely by lay brothers (monks not under holy orders), these granges often generated income for the mother Abbey; sheep rearing for wool figured prominently in their activities and Roystone Grange maintained large flocks over the best part of 200 years, selling fleeces to Flemish merchants.

Excavations have revealed the original grange site directly below a spring and consisting of a hall some 50ft (15m) long. Around the thirteenth and fourteenth centuries this was superseded by a larger, aisled hall at the centre of the terrace. It contained a kitchen, a hall and a byre (or cattle shelter) and measured about 66ft (20m) long by 39ft (12m) wide. Internal timber posts supported a steep-pitched thatched roof and low, drystone walls.

In and around the buildings, numerous artefacts have been unearthed, including metal tools such as knives and sheep-shears, and fragments of locally made pottery jugs. Remains of animal bones suggest the lay brothers liked to eat mutton—hardly surprising in the circumstances!

Work on this fascinating project is being undertaken by Martin Wildgoose of Closes Farm, Kniveton, and Richard Hodges of Sheffield University, under the enthusiastic eye of the present Roystone Grange farmer, Mr.

David Twigg. At the time of writing (Easter 1990), much remains to be done; already the dairy annexe is clear to see, but it is hoped eventually to conserve all the buildings and to signpost them on the ground for the benefit of visitors.

Four hundred metres further down the dale track, low banks run up the hillside on your left. It is thought that these small terraces date from Roman times when they would probably have been delineated by thorn hedges. Farmers living higher up the valley would have grown hardy crops such as oats here—a possible indication of difficult times during the later stages of Romano-British settlement when pressure to increase self-sufficiency resulted in bringing into service land which otherwise would never have been resorted to. Conditions in this upland dale must have been spartan at the best of times, the weather limiting the range and success of crops. It is only because this steep hillside has been abandoned since the fourth century that the terraces, albeit indistinct, exist for us to ponder.

Lower down still are signs of Saxon strip lynchets, but to venture onwards is to risk disillusionment! Ballidon's quarry workings continue to encroach close to these special sites of antiquity—the wholly ugly face of twentieth century exploitation which contravenes the spirit, if not the letter, of National Parks legislation.

You now retrace your steps up the dale, passing through the farmyard of the current Roystone Grange. It is a solid, eighteenth century farmstead which, at my last visit, was beset with a miscellany of livestock, from geese, sheep, chickens and dogs to peacocks and bullocks! An old brick-built cowshed on the left stands close to the foundations of the main original Roman farmhouse—in effect the hub of a small community farming the valley and rearing stock between the second and fourth centuries AD.

The often muddy track gives way to tarmac further up at Roystone Cottages, leading you onto Minninglow Lane—another section of the old drovers' way; although adopted as an unclassified road, it receives very little traffic. You turn left and follow it up to the junction with Parwich Lane, but be sure to stop now and again to gaze back over magnificent views to Minninglow. Two options now confront you: to short-cut speedily back to the start alongside Cobblersnook Plantation, or to proceed on the route as described below. I heartily recommend the latter, for it yields countryside walking of great character and culminates in what I consider to be the most enjoyable stretch of the High Peak Trail.

Walled Cobblersnook Lane undulates temptingly ahead, a rural thoroughfare unchanged in centuries. Beyond Nook Cottage the way rises gently onto Upper Moor. At a fork you keep right, then straight on along an open field boundary to re-enter the old lane at a gate and stile. At the junction with Green Lane you turn right, on the level initially with views left to Aleck Low. A gradual downhill gradient takes you back to the High Peak Trail where a right heading begins the walk's final leg.

Veering round south above Pikehall, vistas to the north are exceptionally extensive in clear weather and there is a distant hint of the High Peak moors on the horizon. The trackbed has grown narrow from the spread of vegetation since the days when trains plied the line; you will undoubtedly be passed by the occasional cyclist, but otherwise the going is delightfully straightforward. Between upper and lower Gotham Granges, the track performs an incredible 80 degree turn—incredible, that is, for a railway! In fact, the Gotham Curve is the tightest on any British line and during its operational period could only be negotiated by locomotives and rolling stock with a short wheelbase; even then a 5mph speed limit was necessary.

From a walker's point of view, railway trackbeds can be a little tiresome. It has to do with a relationship between the pace of travel and the nature of the terrain. Railways were built to accommodate the limitations of trains which can neither deal with appreciable slopes nor bends beyond a certain angle, so progress by foot sometimes seems too slow. This is why I do not consider it right to feature any of the Peak District's railway trails as classic walks on their own, though sections crop up here and there. It may also account for the popularity of cycling which whisks you along at a decent speed. In many respects, however, the High Peak Trail, with its twisting course and frequent cuttings and embankments, is an exception. Perspectives are constantly changing and there is a pastoral intimacy about the line not normally associated with trackbed walking. Chapel Plantation, through which the conclusion of this outing now passes, illustrates this observation well. A woodland grove of considerable beauty, it enfolds you in sun-filtered tranquillity for the last 300m back to the Minninglow car park.

WALK 7: *Four Dales from Hartington*

Start/Finish: Hartington's market square. **Access:** Hartington lies about 3 miles (4.5km) off the A515, half way between Buxton and Ashbourne. Nearest railway station—Matlock. **Distance:** 11 miles (17.5km) **Terrain:** Field tracks, rocky dale and riverside paths—muddy and slippery in wet weather. **Maps:** OS Landranger Sheet 119. Outdoor Leisure White Peak.

North of Dove Dale, the River Dove meanders through equally magnificent limestone country, if a little more expansive and less densely wooded. Several dry tributary valleys, one—Biggin Dale—surprisingly lengthy, provide means of escape from the otherwise relentlessly steep enclosing hillsides that characterise the Dove's middle reaches.

No end of circular tours may be devised to incorporate these side dales, taking you through the most wonderful scenery en route from one block of high ground to another. The following walk was chosen for its exploration of the Dove between Hartington and Milldale, for its foray down the wild and less frequented Biggin Dale, and for the possibility of refreshments around the halfway point at Milldale or Alstonefield.

Hartington, as convenient a place to begin walking as any I know in the White Peak, is described more fully in Walk 8. From the Market Square car park, you set off east and in 100m or so turn right up past the Chapel Book Shop. Ignoring a right fork, you continue ahead past the grandiose youth hostel at Hartington Hall, then branch off right onto a walled field track known as Highfield Lane.

Running across a gently swelling hill of fields for about a mile, this will being you to Dale End, on the public road from Hartington near the entry to Biggin Dale which lies just 100m straight ahead. Biggin itself boasts a Hall, finished in 1642, and a pub, 'The Waterloo'—meeting place for local farmers during the great sheep sale held in a field opposite each November.

A signposted stile marks the path into upper Biggin Dale which passes a sewage plant (a very low key affair!) and sweeps left. The remains of an old lime kiln can be seen just beyond the next stile, then, beyond a mere and signpost at the junction with a minor valley arm, you enter the Biggin Dale Nature Reserve. Exactly what there is to protect may not be immediately apparent as the valley sides seem featureless and uninteresting. Yet even here, delicate lime-loving plants thrive and support their complement of insect life. Lower down the dale, pockets of thin, bushy woodland and the emergence of running water (especially after prolonged rain) create additional habitats for a wide variety of flora and fauna. In such precious places we should all refrain from picking plants, taking away with us instead only photographs of what pleases us.

Top: **Morris dancers at Hartington.**
Bottom: **Beaver Ford footbridge in Beresford Dale.**

Being free from nearby car parks and therefore from trippers too, these less accessible offshoot dales are usually havens of peace and tranquillity. In places, the Biggin Dale path grows awkwardly rocky and moisture acts like a lubricant on the smoothed limestone surfaces, so watch your footing in damp weather!

Slopes to the right are owned by the National Trust, as is the south-eastern top of Wolfscote Hill about 750m away but obscured from view. As the valley deepens, scree, stones and some sizeable boulders litter its floor. Before long there is sighting ahead of rock-ribbed hillsides flanking the as-yet unseen River Dove.

After more tortuous progress, you pass a mine adit, marked 'cave' on the 1:25,000 map, then a miniature side defile on your left, before reaching Biggin Dale's convergence with Beresford Dale. Immediately, the walk's character changes from quiet seclusion to, in all probability, a well peopled thoroughfare—part of the popular and easy hike alongside the chattering, picturesque Dove. Biggin Dale's own watercourse shows its face here, necessitating a stone causeway for pedestrian crossing.

Very soon you reach Iron Tors Cave—worth scrambling up to for excellent views of this dramatic dale intersection—and, 50m beyond, stepping stones across the river. Provided the water level is low enough to use them, they become the key to the walk's return stage, avoiding the need to tread the same ground twice over about 1200m from Coldeaton Bridge. However, should the river be too high, an alternative routing is given.

Well walked and level the path may be, but it is also quite delectable, especially during spring and summer when wild flowers such as the delicate meadow cranesbill, the yellow wild balsam and, higher up on the limestone outcroppings, rock rose and yellow wall pepper brighten the surroundings.

Thin woodland clothes the precipitous east bank around Iron Tors, leading on to Coldeaton Bridge where a side dale joins near a Water Authority building. From here on, you pass through stiles over riverside pasture, shadowing a big meander to reach the road past cottages dominated by the buttress of Shining Tor.

You turn right, then left along Mill Dale. Just over the road bridge stands Lode Mill after which the dale is named. Originally a lead smelting works, it was later used to grind corn and the old mill wheel remains at the rear of the building. I have always found the following kilometre or so of tarmac to Milldale hamlet to be the least prepossessing stretch of this walk—not because the scenery is significantly poorer but because roads, however

minor, were made for wheeled vehicles and progress on foot usually feels doubly slow by comparison.

Milldale is one of those places that are hard to resist, whether or not you are a walker. Cradled in a deep fold of hills at the northern end of Dove Dale, it acts as a fulcrum around which walks swing from all points of the compass. In recent years, cramped riverside parking spaces have been reserved for residents and a new visitors' car park opened a little way up Hope Dale. The result, during holiday periods at least, is considerable congestion, though the volume of visitors is self-limiting: if you've nowhere to stop, the only option is to drive on! Walkers remain blissfully free of such problems!

The little cafe does a brisk trade, winter weekends and all, and you can sit outside if it's fine; I have yet to stop here without encountering other walkers. Milldale's Viator's Bridge (derived from the Latin for 'traveller's') gracefully spans the Dove adjacent to an Information display and public toilets.

You are now faced with the first appreciable climb of the route thus far, and its only steep one. To your right, facing up Hope Dale, is Millway Lane, a traffic-free (except for access) byway that winds uphill to Alstonefield and could well be followed for its full distance. A slightly shorter variant, however, soon turns off left at a signpost and heads for a muscle-stretching slope which relents to cross fields and regain Millway Lane just short of Alstonefield's church. Set amongst trees, it is a largely fifteenth century building containing some interesting oak box pews carved in 1637/8, one of which is associated with the Cotton Family of Beresford Hall (now demolished).

The hillside you have just traversed epitomises the White Peak landscape. An intricate pattern of small fields, whose boundaries have changed little since the Enclosures Act, bears other signs of use by generations of farmers—field corner barns, pathway wall stiles and a dotting of trees providing shade for cattle during the summer.

Alstonefield's shop-cum-cafe or its pub 'The George' would make a good refreshment stop should you find Milldale overrun; there is a car park here too, and a caravan site. Mentioned in the Domesday Survey, Alstonefield retains the kind of timeless village charm that you find all over rural England. Carefully manicured triangular greens, neat limestone houses and the verdant shade of mature trees tempt you to pause awhile and look around before moving on.

The Milldale road is followed to the village outskirts where a decision must be made

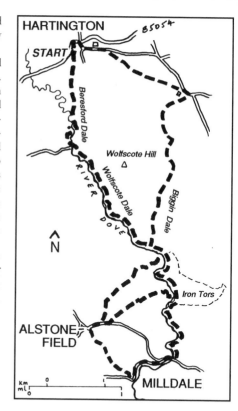

regarding the use of the stepping stones opposite Iron Tors Cave. If they were clear when you passed, you now turn left along a rough, signposted field track and in 400m turn right onto a similar track which ends at a group of farm buildings. From here the onward path is little used but all the wall stiles are there and a little observant navigation will keep you on course. Soon after leaving the barns, you trend left across two fields towards the far side of a shallow valley; swinging right, Wolfscote Dale and the River Dove are gradually revealed. On the steep descent, Iron Tors Cave acts as a landmark by which to locate the stepping stones and the walk continues upstream to the junction with Biggin Dale.

If the stepping stones were covered, or perhaps slippery with ice, they can be avoided by taking the second field track on the left off the Milldale road. Known as Gipsy Lane, this passes Overdale Farm and eventually leads down to Coldeaton Bridge, whence steps are retraced upstream to the Biggin Dale junction.

Walking north up Wolfscote Dale, you pass the tiered ribs of Peaseland Rocks and the great peaked wall of Drabber Tor. Alder scrub and scree line the path and if the Dove is in spate you will be forced, periodically, to scramble higher up the bank to avoid wet feet. The dale has a pronounced 'V' section and narrows excitingly towards a sudden transition into Beresford Dale at Frank's Rock and its little cave—welcome shelter in the rain.

A footbridge gives access to the Dove's west bank, but this route continues ahead through a squeeze stile and out over water meadows to Beaver Ford footbridge at the end of Beresford Lane. Like many footpaths in the White Peak, the onward stretch has been consolidated with stone chippings to withstand the onslaught of human feet, but who would blame anyone for wishing to sample the sylvan delights of Beresford Dale!

Pike Pool, named after a prominent rock finger projecting from the craggy little gorge, is seen at the next footbridge. The Tudor-style tower, now on the opposite side of the river overhung with woodland, is associated with Charles Cotton's fishing pavilion a little farther along but almost hidden from view. Erected in 1674, it became a regular retreat for Cotton and his great friend Izaak Walton, author of *The Compleat Angler* in later editions of which Cotton himself sings the Dove's praises as a trout stream. Their combined, interwoven initials and the legend 'Piscatoribus Sacrum 1674' appear over the doorway.

As you leave Beresford Dale to climb the shoulder of Pennilow, you also bid farewell to the Dove which now twists in incipient oxbows away to the north-west. Linking stiles and crossing a green lane, the rising path provides a splendid retrospective view of Wolfscote Hill. Underfoot conditions are frequently muddy and you are finally deposited—conveniently, perhaps, if you will excuse the pun—by the public toilets next to Hartington's pottery!

Right and below: **Milldale, a picturesque hamlet cradled in a deep fold of hills, makes a popular refreshment halt for walkers.**

WALK 8: *Limestone Peaks of the Upper Dove Valley*

Start/Finish: Hartington's Market Square. **Access:** Hartington stands on the B5054, 2 miles off the A515 Buxton to Ashbourne road. **Distance:** 13 miles (21km)—allow 5 to 6 hours. **Terrain:** Often muddy valley paths and tracks, country lanes and a sharp ascent (optional). **Maps:** OS Landranger Sheet 119. Outdoor Leisure White Peak.

South of Hartington the River Dove winds through dales of legendary beauty. Walking is easy and in almost any weather this Wagnerian landscape of limestone tors, caves, precipitous woodland and babbling water can be enjoyed, free from the discomforts of exposure to the elements experienced on the hills above.

Dove Dale has become enshrined in tourist literature as an obligatory destination for visitors to the White Peak. Its popularity is immense, witness the large car park beneath Thorpe Cloud and the resurfacing of footpaths to cope with the onslaught of human feet. I would not for one minute decry its reputation, yet the River Dove possesses another face—one which, though less intensively dramatic, is worthy of the walker's attention.

In their upper reaches, the Dove and Manifold rivers open out. Unconfined by cliffs or beetling hillsides, they meander quietly through meadows in a great wedge of gentler, rolling land rising to the distant moorland horizon of Morridge and Axe Edge. As we shall discover midway through this walk, the limestone scenery holds some surprises up its sleeve but there is a greater sense of freedom here (and certainly better views) than in the deep and sometimes claustrophobic valleys further south.

Hartington combines the mellow charm of a traditional Peakland village with the amenities visitors have come to expect in a centre so well positioned for exploring the White Peak. You really have to see it out of season when the coaches and holidaymakers have gone to appreciate a history that dates back seven centuries to its emergence as an important local market town. Its buildings of limestone and gritstone are typical of the Peak, as is the village mere (or duckpond). On elevated ground to the east stands Hartington Hall, put up in the seventeenth century, extended in the nineteenth and now a rather grand youth hostel. The church, too, is impressive in its own way, its dark, battlemented tower overseeing the goings-on beneath.

Endowed with cafes, hotels, shops, a garage, banks and public conveniences, Hartington is an ideal spot from which to set off walking.

A lot of people know this, so arrive early if you want parking space at popular times! Once on the trail, however, you will meet few other souls.

From the village pond you walk west along the access road to J.M. Nuttall's milk processing plant. This, sadly, is Derbyshire's last surviving cheese factory, manufacturing a range of plain, veined and flavoured Stiltons. You used to be able to look round but the public is no longer admitted, though the cheeses are on sale in a dairy shop by the mere.

As signed, you turn right in front of the factory and from its car park follow stiles across fields to a footbridge over the River Dove. The first of several moderate little climbs ensues as you scale the valley side and link more stiles to emerge on a country lane at Lower House Farm, just short of Sheen hamlet. Turn right here and in about 100m you cross the second stile on your left to make a beeline for the minor road near Moorhouse Farm. I have always found the stiles through fields down towards the River Manifold to be awkward but that may change; in any case you soon find yourself immediately above a bridge spanning the river.

Having thus traversed farmland separating the Dove and Manifold, you now follow the latter north. The going can be muddy and you

Facing page: **Hartington Church.**

Above right: **A wayside barn in the Manifold valley.**

Below right: **The upper Dove valley from just above Longnor.**

may need to consult the 1:25,000 map to confirm the path line, though by playing 'spot the stile' the way ahead unfolds clearly enough. Depending on the season of your visit, birds will keep you company—skylarks, peewits and wheatears perhaps—while clumps of ox-eye daisy and ragged robin brighten the pathside here and there.

Pool Farm is passed to the left and the little tributary stream crossed by stone bridge. Beyond a walled lane encountered soon after, the path continues without complication all the way to Longnor. Drystone walls march over low hills south-east of the village—a lovely sight—and for a time you walk close to the Manifold itself. Then a right turn from a stile takes you up to Folds End Farm whose access road leads to the centre of Longnor, set on a ridge dividing the upper Dove and Manifold valleys.

In common with most other villages in the Peak's western sector, Longnor's prosperity, at its height as a focus for a prosperous farming community during the mid-nineteenth century, declined with the subsequent depression in agriculture. Even its coaching trade, based on the turnpike crossroads which it straddles, was destined not to last. The railway never came here and Longnor seemed set to pass into obscurity.

In 1977, however, the village became a Conservation Area and the Peak Park authorities have undertaken much worthwhile restoration work. Craft workshops have been set up (take a look at 'Sculpture' in the old Market Hall) and the community is sensing a new lease of life as a touring base and a centre for arts and crafts.

A scale of tolls charged on market and fair days and dated 1903 appears on the Market Hall's exterior above the sloping, cobbled square. From here a narrow, paved alley—Chapel Street—will take you up steps, left across Church Street and soon a footpath sign directs walkers right by a bungalow estate. (You could simply continue ahead up the B5053, missing out this short, tarmac-avoiding loop). Dropping down a scrub-covered bank, you pick up the track from Underhill Farm which rises to a road junction where you fork left towards Hollinsclough.

Already the crowning features of this walk are in full view—an array of curious peaks, mountainous in shape if not in stature. These striking conical eminences are the fossilised remnants of coral reefs, in essence no different from their living counterparts in today's warm tropical seas. Three hundred million years ago (a bemusingly abstract statistic!) these undersea forms were laid down at the edge of a vast, shallow lagoon stretching east to the

position of Eyam, Bakewell and Matlock. The reef knolls continue south as Hitter Hill, High Wheeldon and outcrop throughout Dove Dale.

Shortly after sharp right and left bends in the lane not far from Hollinsclough, a track angles back directly towards the curved ridge of Chrome (pronounced 'Croom') Hill. There is no access to its slopes and in any case until you reach a footbridge over the Dove you are on the wrong side of the river.

On reaching the by-road a short distance ahead, Parkhouse Hill, most distinctive of the reef knolls from the majority of angles, rears tantalisingly above you. The walk crosses its southern flanks, diverging away from the road towards Glutton Grange, and a temptation to scale the peak may be too strong to resist! The landowning farmer at Glutton Grange, reluctant to fence off the hill from fossil-hunting geologists and less responsible members of the walking fraternity, nevertheless discourages access by polite notice. Needless to day, views from the rocky little 'arrête' are sensational!

At a wall stile you drop right over a stream and meet the B5053. The stile directly opposite and a left-trending path lead you via a distinctive groove above Glutton Dale to the rim of Hitter Hill. Whilst regaining your breath and before proceeding across enclosures to Earl Sterndale, it is worth glancing back to savour the profiles of Parkhouse and Chrome hills. Were they twice their height and wooded round their base, they would indeed be serious competition for Thorpe Cloud and Dove Dale. As it is, the modest elevation of these extraordinary land forms means they lack prominence in views from afar.

Earl Sterndale, a long, grey-stoned village whose links by family association with King Sterndale beyond Brierlow Bar reach back to medieval times, is no longer the isolated upland outpost it once was. Close by to the north, the huge Dowlow quarry complex has transformed the landscape and forced the National Park boundary into an accommodating loop.

You leave round the back of the 'Quiet

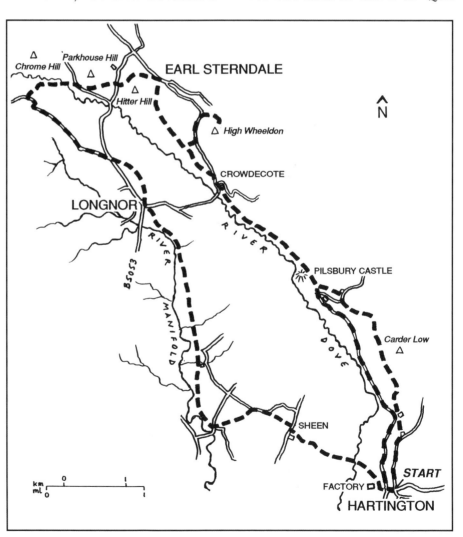

Woman' pub (her headlessness the wishful thinking of a former owner!) and walk up over pasture to attain the rougher ridge top (a signed footpath diversion is in force here, not shown on maps). Following a wall round, there are good views over the Dove valley to Longnor, but soon attention to the ground is called for as you descend to a bridleway.

Beyond Underhill Farm a stiled field path heads for Crowdecote, converging with the country lane. However, an ascent of High Wheeldon is strongly recommended if time and inclination permit. This is achieved by turning left up the road to a stile and National Trust sign on the right. It is perfectly feasible to attack the steep hillside in a south-easterly direction. You will pass Fox Hole Cave on the way up; archaeological finds from the series of chambers and passages within include animal bones and other remains from Neolithic and Palaeolithic times, but the entrance is kept locked in the interests of posterity.

A more proper line of ascent takes the wall-side path and doubles back at the Wheeldon Trees track. Either way, the 1383-ft (422m) summit will be attained—in fact not an isolated pyramid as perceived from the north-west but the sharpened prow of a broad ridge. As a memorial to the men of Derbyshire and Staffordshire killed in World War II, the hill was given to the nation, later to pass into the stewardship of the National Trust. If you are blessed with good visibility there is an incomparable 360-degree panorama from the OS pillar.

Back at the road, 15 minutes gently downhill will bring you to Crowdecote. Just past the Packhorse Inn you turn left along a walled farm track and out through herb-rich meadows close to the River Dove. A mile on, the way rises behind Pilsbury Castle. The motte-and-bailey earthworks are well defined and are thought to have incorporated the mounds and ditches of a much earlier Iron Age fortification. Perched atop a limestone spur, it is an inspiring situation for a defensive position: little wonder its history is so long!

A track is now joined to Pilsbury farmstead, whence the valley road can be followed right back to Hartington—just over 2 miles (3.5km). An alternative route making the most of high ground starts by forking left at Pilsbury and turning right through a stile after a sharp left bend in the road. For a short while you are treading the old salt way to Bakewell and Chesterfield but you soon branch right past wall corners and the remains of a lead mine.

Flanking Carder Low and with wide views to your right, the path nears outcrops resembling a limestone pavement—an uncommon sight in the Peak District. A hairpin bend in the track above Bank Top Farm is closely followed by arrival at Hide Lane, 800m from Hartington's church.

Glutton Grange (centre) and Earl Sterndale (above), from the summit of Parkhouse Hill.

WALK 9: *The Roaches, Lud's Church and Hen Cloud*

Start/Finish: Lay-by at Rockhall. **Access:** 1 mile (1.5km) by minor road from Upper Hulme, itself 3 miles (5km) north-east of Leek on the A53. Nearest railway stations—Buxton and Macclesfield. **Distance:** 8½ miles (14km)—allow about 4 hours. **Terrain:** Mostly firm going along a gritstone edge, through steep woodland and up a minor summit. A little country road walking. **Maps:** OS Landranger Sheets 118 and 119. Outdoor Leisure White Peak.

Unlike the clearly structured escarpments of the eastern gritstone edges, the south-western sector of the Peak Park is folded into complex arrangements of basins, ridges (locally 'minns') and outcrops called 'clouds' (after the Celtic 'clud' for rock). Rising abruptly from the Cheshire Plain, it is a landscape of secret valleys and unexpected rock architecture—a countryside haunted by myth and legend.

Dominating this walk is the geology of the Roaches syncline, a giant 'V' formed by Ramshaw Rocks and The Roaches, with Hen Cloud at the apex. Bold crags face softer, rolling lowlands, announcing the start of true hill country, for these sombre western moors are as great a force to be reckoned with as their better known northern counterparts. Reservoirs and forestry plantings represent man's most recent relationship with the land, but layers of history date back to the passage of Roman legionnaires en route to and from Buxton—Aquae Arnemetiae—along the same roadway north from Leek that in all probability whisked you to the start of this modern-day saunter.

At the southern end of The Roaches (derived from the French 'rochers' for rocks), the minor road from Upper Hulme is widened to accommodate a row of parked cars. A gate leads into a rising track towards the now derelict Rockhall cottage, once a gamekeeper's house and more recently the home of a local eccentric 'Doug, Lord of The Roaches': at my last visit it was in a dangerous condition and had been boarded up. Skirting left of the wildly overgrown garden, you pass through a wall gap into a pine-shaded slope of massive, grey-brown boulders. Ahead, you need to locate a flight of steep stone steps leading through a narrow gully between crags; these take you halfway to the top of the double-tiered edge. (In fact, lower down the hill a third tier is effectively added to this edge in the shape of Five Clouds, a less extensive row of crags set close above the road).

Before continuing, note the natural gritstone 'seat' on the left, visited by Queen Mary's mother in 1872. To your right rears the Great Slab bearing the late Don Whillans' challenging rock-climbing route 'The Sloth'—so named because of the need to hang upside down when negotiating the overhang! Some of the Peak's finest and most sustained climbing is to be found at The Roaches, and its proximity to road access endows it with great popularity.

Walking on along the terrace beneath a con-

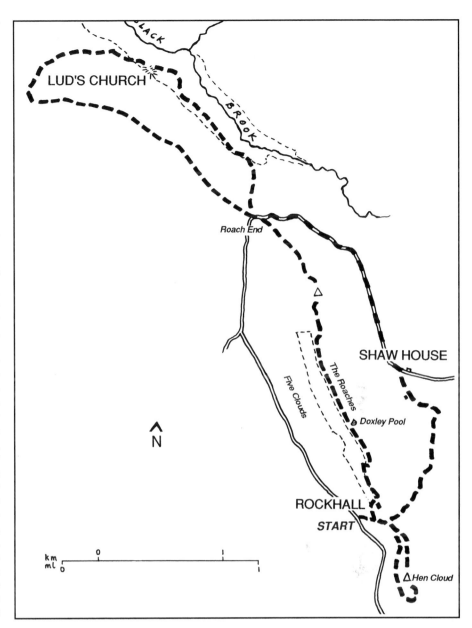

fusion of sheer slabs riven by cracks, chimneys and overhanging pinnacles, you turn right beside a broken wall and fence to ascend a breach of loose rocks in the otherwise continuous upper tier of gritstone. Emerging onto the summit promenade gives you a tremendous sense of airy space, with good views back to Ramshaw Rocks and Hen Cloud, though better yet lies in store!

Climbing gently along the rocky edge top, you pass Doxey Pool, mentioned in the Domesday Survey and probably named after a local inhabitant. In the absence of any stream, it is a surprising feature to come across in such a location, but a small swath of muddy peat overlays the sandstone here, preventing normal drainage of rainwater.

A gradual dip and climb round wind-streaked, cross-bedded rocks brings you to the OS trig pillar—1658ft (505m) above sea level and a marvellous panoramic viewpoint. Its praises were sung back in 1730 by the author of *The Compleat History of Staffordshire* who declared: 'Here are also vast Rocks which surprise with Admiration, called Henclouds and Leek Roches. They are of so great a Height and afford such stupendous Prospects that one could hardly believe they were anywhere to be found but in Picture.' Shutlingsloe's distinctive wedge-shaped profile (somewhat optimistically dubbed 'The Matterhorn of the Peak') is prominent to the north-west, while to the south in contrast glitter the waters of distant Tittesworth Reservoir.

I came here last one wild winter's day. A north-westerly gale swept heavy showers through the Dane Gap towards Leek, obliterating all in dense canopies of white-grey precipitation: you simply kept a weather eye open up-wind and awaited the inevitable darkening horizon. Pregnant with moisture, the storm was soon overhead, squally gusts of wind and the first stinging raindrops sending me scuttling vainly for shelter behind the nearest rocks.

A fifteen-minute descent through heather past Bearstone Rock (the resemblance eludes me I'm afraid, but it is one of several gritstone outcrops sculpted by the elements) brings you to Roach End and re-acquaintance with the minor road from which you set out. Should a short-cut be indicated, the onward route makes a loop returning to Roach End so simply follow the road east as described further below.

The ridge continues ahead as Back Forest but forms a step here, giving fine views to the north and west. Directly across the road a stiled, concessionary path heads on for over a mile down the broad ridge crest past rocky out-

crops, eventually reaching a signposted footpath intersection. (Halfway along, a path short-cuts down right to Forest Wood should you prefer to leave the ridge early.)

Our onward route swings right, but not far away to the south-west stands Swythamley Hall, rebuilt by the Brocklehurst family in the nineteenth century; its private zoo once released a number of wallabies into the local countryside.

Having reached the walk's farthest point, you now follow the path to the right alongside a wall, then over hillside to Castle Cliff Rocks. By keeping to the upper track where it forks, and descending steps from a narrow entrance on the right, you will find yourself in the remarkable chasm known as Lud's Church. Its proportions take you by surprise—indeed, its existence is unguessed at until you are upon it. For years it was quite difficult to locate, but the National Park authorities have improved access since acquiring the Roaches Estate in 1975.

A rift of such magnitude in an otherwise unexceptional hillside must be regarded as a freak geological occurrence. Walls 50ft (15m)

high and 20ft (6m) apart envelop you in a womb of dank, vegetated shade; hedged in by tree roots, ferns and weirdly shaped rocks, it takes little imagination to invoke visions of spirits and mysterious goings-on in less rational times than our own. This was reputedly a secret place of worship for the fourteenth-century Wycliff Lollards (hence 'Church') and was named after the pastor Walter de Lud-Auk, one of Wycliff's followers. There are also associations with the medieval poem 'Sir Gawain and the Green Knight', recent research suggesting that Lud's Church is the legendary Green Chapel, and Swythamley Hall the Green Knight's castle. The Peak District held many wonders for Victorian tourists whose perceptions of natural phenomena were coloured by the romantic language of the time: how hearts must have quickened at entering this miniature gorge, one of the area's 'sights'.

Climbing out into daylight again, you stay with the upper contouring path above steepnesses through Forest Wood, joining the main Gradbach path uphill rockily to Roach End. Although used by motorists, the road makes for pleasant walking too as it curves south-east high above the valley of Black Brook. Just beyond a left bend and before Shaw House, you leave the tarmac for gates on the right into a track past ruinous Shawtop. On over a stile and along by a fence you reach the access track from Summerhill, turning right and continuing in the same direction to cross the upper reaches of the River Churnet.

Arriving at a grassy saddle between The Roaches and Hen Cloud, there is no mistaking a clear (concessionary) ridge path rising to the 1345-ft (410m) conical summit of Hen Cloud ('High Rock'), a hill which always puts me in mind of Roseberry Topping in the North York Moors. It forms a marvellous finale to the walk, and an excellent viewpoint not only to the skyward thrust of Ramshaw Rocks less than a mile away to the north-east, but back along the foreshortened serrations of The Roaches and south to Tittesworth Reservoir.

Predictably, a rock-climbers' trod weaves down beneath the cliffs, but more straightforward progress is made by continuing south, down into thin woods, and veering right onto the Roaches House drive. Rather than resorting to the road, I recommend the narrow path forking right across steep hillside a little way below the base of the crags: it delivers you back to the grassy saddle from where a track angles down to the car parking lay-by.

Left: **Looking back along the Roaches syncline; the farthest prow of rock is Hen Cloud.**

WALK 10: *Arbor Low, Bradford Dale and the High Peak Trail*

Start/Finish: Parsley Hay. **Access:** Just off the A515 approx. 10 miles (16km) south-east of Buxton. Nearest railway stations—Buxton and Matlock. **Distance:** 12 miles (19.5km)—allow about 6 hours. **Terrain:** A mix of country lanes, farm tracks, field, riverside and dale paths, and a dismantled railway trackbed. **Maps:** OS Landranger Sheet 119. Outdoor Leisure White Peak.

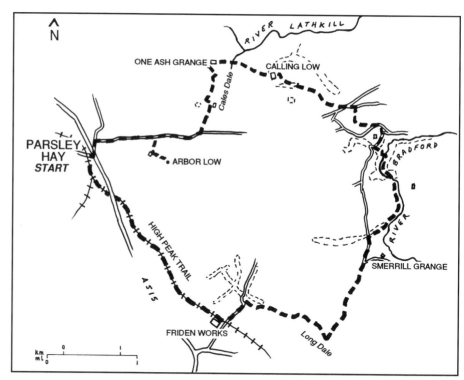

The car park, picnic site and National Park cycle hire centre at Parsley Hay Wharf south-east of Buxton, draw in many visitors. Were it not for the existence of the High Peak and Tissington trails, however, fewer people by far would explore this rolling plateau more than 1000ft (305m) above sea level, for footpaths are relatively scarce. It is a marvellously open landscape of drystone walls and wooded knolls, dissected here and there by limestone dales—some waterless, others bearing rivers of great beauty such as the Lathkill and the Bradford.

The cinder trackbed of the dismantled Cromford and High Peak Railway (as well as that of the Ashbourne to Buxton line known as the Tissington Trail, covered elsewhere in this book) provides an ideal cycling route for family groups and others to whom speed is unimportant—hence the growing popularity of cycle hire at Parsley Hay. Walkers, too, can enjoy a gently unfolding countryside free from route-finding distractions, as the last stage of this walk will demonstrate.

One of the White Peak's principle attributes as a walking region is its intrinsic diversity. Within the span of a dozen miles, this itinerary will lead you through some of its best scenery, largely unbeset by the crowds that descend upon well known beauty spots where there is easy road access.

It is a walk of contrasts, offering a combination of shelter from and exposure to the elements—whether that means wind and cold or sunshine and heat, extremes of which can always pose a threat. Farmland may look innocuous enough, but at this elevation the weather is capable of rapid change and unexpected severity.

Unless a detour is made to Youlgreave in the Bradford valley (not particularly far off route), nowhere is passed that will slake a thirst or satisfy a healthy appetite. With this in mind, I recommend you pack snacks and a picnic and plenty to drink. In winter especially, go prepared with a weather forecast and appropriate protective clothing.

From the Parsley Hay car park there is a little road walking involved to get under way; care is needed crossing the A515 as traffic speeds downhill from both directions. You take the road directly opposite towards Moneyash and in no more than 250m turn right up Long Rake. Half a mile further on, having passed a plantation at the brow of a hill, you will see

a sign for Arbor Low directing you along Upper Oldham Farm's track on the right. There is a fee for car parking (payable at an honesty box by the farmhouse at my last visit), but walkers can march straight up through the farmyard, veering left over a sloping field and crossing a stile to the henge site.

If you were expecting standing stones, in the mould of an Avebury or a Castlerigg perhaps, you may experience a little initial disappointment. The 47 perimeter and 3 central stones all lie horizontal yet, nevertheless, their arrangement within a 250-ft (76m) diameter circular bank and ditch—a typical 'henge' layout—is hugely impressive when it is remembered they date back 3500 to 4000 years to the late Neolithic/early Bronze Age period. When mist shrouds the plateau, as it often does, Arbor Low assumes an extraordinary air of mystery, particularly if you are fortunate to have it all to yourself. In the low sun of dawn or dusk, the stones—pitted and scoured by constant exposure to the elements—seem to glow with an ancient inner fire. Little is known of the site's ritualistic function, so imaginations are free to roam!

It is certainly worth scaling the bank for a bird's eye view of this, the Peak District's largest stone circle. From there you can also contemplate Gib Hill tumulus, situated about 300m to the south-west; it is the region's biggest round barrow and excavations near its top 140 years ago unearthed a small burial chamber containing a cremation and a food vessel.

Similar relics were found in a barrow on the banks of Arbor Low.

Having absorbed what you will of this splendidly positioned prehistoric monument, steps are retraced back to the Long Rake road. Within half a mile to the right, you take a left turn into the cattle-grid entrance of Cales Farm access road which swings downhill, dips left of the farm buildings and proceeds ahead to One Ash Grange. Beyond the camping barn loft (one splendid way of giving a new lease of life to unused shelter), you pass pig styes and a curious grotto behind the farmhouse and reach a stile at the end of the dutch barn. Across pasture lies a fence stile where you drop through a rocky cleft into Cales Dale.

Almost immediately you divert right, across the ravine to a stepped path mounting the steep dale side then easing off through large grange pastures to Calling Low Farm. There are waymark posts and beyond the farm, the path—though angling constantly over a matrix of fields—is well walked. I have always been struck by the elegant patterns formed by walls and stands of trees in the vicinity of Calling Low—as if the landscape achieves within a square mile a kind of distillation of all those aesthetic qualities associated with the White Peak. Bee Low Wood dominates the skyline ahead until you veer right, missing its eastern end to emerge at the Long Rake road by some smaller enclosures.

A short distance along the road to the west, its presence betrayed by white dust or slurry (depending on the weather), stands Long Rake Calcite Works. As elsewhere in the National Park, calcite is mined and transported away by lorries whose trundling presence on narrow country roads is less than welcome, to the visiting public at least. Calcite itself is a white (or colourless) mineral found here in limestone and used in the manufacture of cement, plaster, paint, glass and fertilizer and one has to accept that its extraction provides valuable jobs.

From the car park and picnic area a little way along Moor Lane—the right fork towards Youlgreave—a signed track is followed south, swinging east above a wood to meet a road lower down. Off the bend ahead, another path cuts down through parkland near Lomberdale Hall to reach the lower road from Youlgreave to Middleton. Lomberdale Hall was the home of an eminent local archaeologist, Thomas Bateman. Over a period of 20 years he excavated some 500 barrows—his own grave is crowned by a Bronze Age urn—and most of his discoveries are on show in Sheffield's Western Park Museum.

Turning right along the road towards Middleton for some 400m will bring you to a signposted path on the left descending a wooded side valley; it drops in zig-zags to a bridge over the River Bradford at an old, overgrown weir.

Contrasts with the open country already traversed could hardly be drawn more sharply. Here you are protected from wind and weather by steep-sided woodland through which the River Bradford, dilated into dammed fish ponds, heads sluggishly east to join forces with the Lathkill at Alport, the Wye near Congreave and the Derwent at Rowsley. You turn right along a broad riverside track (part of the Limestone Way coming in from Youlgreave) and pass the remains of old sheep wash pens. Pretty Middleton village lies up a crag-fringed path on the right, but the walk stays upstream with the river which henceforward reverts to its natural status as a mere stream. A narrow footbridge takes you over and up steps, but where the crags recede you fork right and re-cross on the massive stone slabs of an ancient clapper bridge.

With Hopping Farm on the hillside to your left, the route links a sequence of wall stiles parallel to Rowlow Brook, the infant Bradford. Beyond a small enclosure and roofless barn you cross a farm lane and continue ahead in the same direction until encountering low limestone cliffs. Here you strike off right into a little wooded gorge; a stile in the left wall corner

near the top is the key to attaining the by-road—Weaddow Lane—leading south to a hairpin bend near Smerrill Grange.

Without changing direction, you take to a stony 'hollow way'—possibly the line of the very old Peakway track—off the bend's apex. It mounts a dry valley between Gratton Moor and high ground surrounding Kenslow Knoll; a half mile or so hemmed in to field bottoms where, in summer, cattle congregate lazily, interrupted only occasionally by passing walkers. Once beneath high tension power lines you pass a barn and a mere and at a gate turn sharp right to undulate above rocky outcrops flanking Long Dale. Opposite Smerrill Moor the path eventually ducks down to the left and shadows the mixed woodland of Bolderstone Plantation to the Youlgreave Road. You are close to the line of a Roman Road but its promise as an explorable feature on maps is not fulfilled on the ground where only the alignment of field walls gives any hint of its former existence here. Certainly no rights of way exist over farmland along its course.

The High Peak Trail at Friden picnic site near the old brickworks lies 500m up the road

to the left. From here onwards you will be tramping the cinder trackbed of the erstwhile Cromford and High Peak Railway, designed to connect the Cromford Canal with the Peak Forest Canal at Whaley Bridge. Opened in 1830, it was originally conceived as a canal—hence the stations called 'wharves'—but would become one of Britain's earliest railway operations. Passengers and freight were hauled by horses at first, with stationary steam engines powering a cable system on the steeper inclines.

Over the years, the fortunes of trackside quarries declined and the railway's usefulness waned. The line from Friden to Parsley Hay—the final leg of this walk—remained open until 1967. Four years later, $17\frac{1}{2}$ miles (28km) of track running within the National Park was purchased and designated as a trail for use by the general public. Not only are there old railway buildings and other engineering features of interest in their own right, but the line weaves a scenic course through the heart of the White Peak. Its uniform walking surface may not appeal to everyone, though fine landscape views are ample compensation.

A section of the High Peak Trail east of Parsley Hay.

Cyclists use it too, more especially between March and November when cycle hire centres are open.

And so begins a short, imaginary, train journey! Blakemore Plantation, a narrow shelter belt, is closely followed by a sharp-angled bend into a cutting. Ahead, you enter the 47m long Newhaven Tunnel beneath the A515; over the portals at each end are original Cromford and High Peak Railway Company plaques dating from 1825. The northern one is more elaborate and bears the Latin inscription 'Divina Palladis Arte' (by the Divine Skill of Palle, Greek Goddess of Engineering). Emerging from the gloom, there is an opening out towards hills enclosing the upper Dove to the west. Soon the Tissington Trail converges from the left and in a few hundred metres you will have arrived back at Parsley Hay.

Facing page: **The view downstream from medieval Conksbury Bridge.**

Below: **One of the old weirs forming fish ponds in the River Bradford near Youlgreave.**

WALK 11: *Moneyash, Lathkill Dale and Youlgreave*

Start/Finish: Chapel Street car park, Moneyash. **Access:** Moneyash is situated about 1 mile (1.5km) east of the A515 between Buxton and Ashbourne. Nearest railway station—Buxton. **Distance:** 12 miles (19km)—allow about 5 hours. **Terrain:** Dale and field paths, often muddy; 1 mile of road walking. **Maps:** OS Landranger Sheet 119. Outdoor Leisure White Peak.

Right: **Moneyash—improbably isolated on limestone uplands.**

Below: **In the rocky upper recesses of Lathkill Dale.**

Charles Cotton, in a contribution to Izaak Walton's *The Compleat Angler* published in 1676, writes of the River Lathkill '. . . it is, by many degrees the purest and most transparent stream that I ever yet saw, either at home or abroad; and breeds, 'tis said, the reddest and best Trouts in England.'

Three hundred years later, little seems to have changed, although at my last visit in the summer of 1990, water levels had fallen to such an extent that the river bed had become choked with vegetation. Given adequate rainfall, however, the Lathkill's crystal clarity—and the wildlife this sustains—transcends that of any other river in Derbyshire. For the reason we must look to Carboniferous Limestone which forms both river bed and gathering grounds, filtering out impurities.

Lathkill Dale is incomparably beautiful and for many walkers—myself included—a jaunt downstream from its dry upper reaches near Moneyash to its confluence with the River Bradford, followed by a return over adjacent hillsides to the south, will always provide a day out to remember. There is much to see along the way, from limestone crags and caves, fishing weirs, ancient bridges and lead mining relics, to Peakland villages, deep woods and historic farms.

If required, the walk may be shortened at several points or, if transport can be arranged, taken as a linear route from Moneyash to Alport, leaving out the return leg altogether. Refreshments are obtainable off-route at Over Haddon and at Youlgreave, just beyond the halfway mark.

Moneyash ('many ash trees'), improbably isolated on limestone uplands between Hartington and Bakewell, probably owes its very existence to a bed of clay, around the perimeter of which—at its junction with the limestone—rise some two dozen springs. Before the advent of piped supplies, clay-lined ponds, or 'meres', often provided the main source of drinking water—occasionally for humans but more usually for stock. One such—Fere Mere—can be seen just south of Moneyash's central crossroads. The dressing of the nearby well each May is a form of thanksgiving, acknowledging the gift of water in a region where it is often scarce.

In days past when rapid communications

and transport had yet to develop, isolated villages like Moneyash needed to generate a trading income in order to survive. Small industries here once included rope and candle manufacturing, quarrying, mere building and, most importantly, lead mining, the latter with its own Barmote Court arbitrating in disputes and administering legal aspects of the operation.

Signs of widespread strip cultivation in fields around Moneyash provide further evidence of a fierce self-sufficiency. A village market held on the Spring and Summer Bank Holidays represents a modern revival of an old weekly market dating back to 1340.

There is a National Park car park in Chapel Street and from the village green crossroads you turn left past the 'Hobbit', following the B5055 Bakewell road for about 600m down to a hollow (the lower end of tiny Bagshaw Dale). A stile on the right marks the true beginning of the walk, although you have to cross two fields before entering the shallow defile of Lathkill Dale.

Almost immediately, limestone buttresses crowd in on the path and you are negotiating boulders brought down by workings in the now disused Ricklow Quarry on your left. This was the source of the once fashionable 'Derbyshire Figured Marble', actually a crinoidal limestone which is highly decorative when polished to reveal its delicate tracery.

Above: **Springtime on the River Lathkill, downstream from Over Haddon.**

Below: **Autumn in Lathkill Dale—one of the best seasons for a visit.**

Owing to the abundance of lime-loving plants and fungi—including herb robert, the pale wood violet, wood avens, Solomon's seal and wood sanicle—158 acres of upper Lathkill Dale were designated a National Nature Reserve in 1972, the first to be established in the Peak Park. It is, of course, incumbent upon us all to respect the delicate flora and to refrain from picking or damaging specimens.

Until you reach Lathkill Head Cave, opposite Parson's Tor, from which the unfortunate Rev. Robert Lomas, vicar of Moneyash, fell to his death in 1776, the valley remains a dry one. However, during the rainy winter months (assuming our traditional weather patterns have not been permanently upset by global warming) the infant River Lathkill issues forth from the cave as the clearest water imaginable, to begin its journey east towards a confluence with the River Bradford at Alport.

Dotted with small trees and curving south between higher, grassier hillsides, the valley reaches a junction with Cales Dale at a footbridge. Ahead lies woodland of mainly ash and elm, sketchy at first but one of the enduring delights of Lathkill Dale, especially in spring and autumn. Just round the next bend appears Lathkill Falls, unimpressive by waterfall yardsticks but interesting as a bed of 'tufa', organic material petrified by the passage of lime-bearing water over long periods of time. Rocky side dales—to the right, Calling Low Dale with its ancient rock shelter, to the left a sinuous passage up onto the plateau at Haddon Grove—diverge from the site of the old Carter's corn mill. Improved from a knobbly, awkward trod in the upper dale to a firm landrover track through Palmerston Wood, the way now permits a quicker stride.

Rich veins of lead-bearing ore attracted miners to this quiet riverside from the thirteenth century to the nineteenth and during the latter years when activity reached its zenith the River Lathkill itself was controlled to avoid flooding of the underground workings. Various shaft hollows occur in Palmerston Wood, but the remains of Mandale Mine at the junction with Twin Dales will gladden the eye of anyone fascinated by industrial archaeology. The leat and ruined aqueduct to your right brought water from upstream to drive pump waterwheels and fragments of the pumping house are still discernible in the undergrowth.

At a gate beyond, you leave the Nature Reserve and follow a straight pathway to Lathkill Lodge, an old mill connected to Over Haddon by a steep and twisting lane, unsuitable for motors at its bottom end. Over Haddon is worth a detour if you have time. There are pub, shop, cafe, car park and a newly developed Crafts Centre. Views from this elevated position at 800ft (244m) on the limestone plateau are excellent, particularly south across Lathkill Dale to Youlgreave and the moors beyond.

Downstream of Bubbling Springs, the dale opens out and becomes vaguely reminiscent of parkland, with coots and moorhens frequenting river banks bright with marsh marigold. What began life as a subterranean stream has graduated to the status of a broad and graceful river. Fishing weirs create ideal conditions for anglers by impounding fish and oxygenating the water, and plant life abounds.

At picturesque Conksbury Bridge you turn right on the minor road, then left through a stile to resume riverside progress. A lane is crossed below Raper Lodge (Raper Mine,

across the dale, yielded fluorspar) and a series of small meadows passed through by stiles, just back from the water's edge which is private land.

And so, at the residential settlement of Alport, you reach the end of Lathkill Dale. Youlgreave, our next immediate objective, lies just over ½ mile up the westward heading road, but a more pleasant routing by far is to continue the riverside theme for a little longer. To achieve this, you cross the B5056 to a white gate and follow a rough track over a farm bridge to the right, passing Rhiens Tor on your way beside the River Bradford. Below Bradford village—effectively an extension of Youlgreave—you cross the footbridge and walk up to Youlgreave's main street, an elongated affair which someone dubbed 'England's longest car park'!

Youlgreave's church, its imposing Perpendicular tower almost obstructing the roadway, is one of the oldest in the county. Both nave and font are Norman and the latter's integrated stoop (or circular bowl) for oil is thought to be unique in England. If you walked left along the narrow street, you would pass the mullioned Old Hall, built in 1656, and, unseen to its rear, Old Hall Farm which predates it by some 25 years. A nineteenth century, three-storey shop built for the local Co-operative Society now houses the youth hostel. Youlgreave is celebrated for the quality of its well-dressing, begun in 1829 on the establishment of the village's own water company and now extended to 5 wells in all.

Should you have diverted to explore or seek refreshment, the onward route turns right up Moor Lane, a little used by-road that climbs for a mile onto the upland plateau to a car

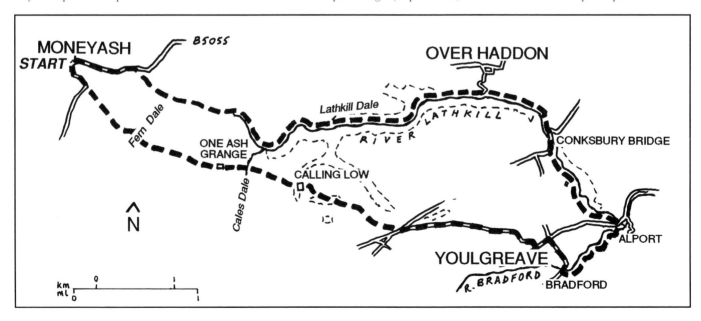

park and the Long Rake road. Whilst climbing, magnificent views open out round the entire southern half of the compass—an open prospect that contrasts sharply with Lathkill Dale's close-range intimacy.

A wall stile opposite the road junction starts you off on a westward, cross-field course defined by further stiles. Close to Bee Low over cultivated ground at first, you soon drop gently through the eastern end of Low Moor Plantation to Calling Low Farm, set in a landscape of drystone walls, pasture and shelter belts so typical of the White Peak.

The path now makes a beeline downhill for Cales Dale and presents you with the walk's only steep gradients; steps have halted erosion on the partly wooded daleside. Ascending a rocky cleft on the opposite bank, you soon arrive at One Ash Grange, one of several monastic farms—or 'granges'—in the area. Their role was to manage vast sheep runs on these rich grasslands, long before the Enclosures Act created the complex web of walls we take for granted today. One Ash was given to the Cistercian house of Roche Abbey in Yorkshire by the Avenell family in the twelfth century, but its remoteness led to monks from the mother Abbey being sent here to do penance!

A farm track takes you unequivocally back towards the walk's conclusion at Moneyash. Fern Dale, a minor offshoot of upper Lathkill Dale, is provided with stiles, whereafter you join a walled lane to the public road at Manor House Farm. Straight ahead lies Fere Mere, the village green and Chapel Street car park.

Bee Low—a landscape of drystone walls and open pasture.

WALK 12: *Bakewell and Haddon Hall*

Start/Finish: Bakewell. **Access:** On the River Wye west of Chesterfield at the intersection of the A6, A619 and B5055. Nearest railway stations—Matlock and Grindleford. **Distance:** 7 miles (11km)—allow 3 hours plus time in Bakewell and Haddon Hall. **Terrain:** Hillside lanes and tracks with an initial ascent, then a riverside path, often muddy. **Maps:** OS Landranger Sheet 119. Outdoor Leisure White Peak.

*Facing page: **The River Wye at Bakewell** and . . .Above: . . . **its community of well fed ducks!***

This relatively modest classic walk, with only one ascent, allows plenty of time for browsing around Bakewell and visiting Haddon Hall. Even so, within its short length there is a surprising variety of scenery, from mixed hillside woodland to a delightful path beside the meandering Wye.

Although the Peak Park is encroached upon by the great conurbations of Sheffield and Manchester for whose populations it represents a welcome retreat to fresh air and countryside, there are few settlements of any size actually within its boundary. Situated at the centre of the White Peak, Bakewell qualifies as the largest town and houses the headquarters of the Peak Park Joint Planning Board.

The town's origins, here at a natural crossing point over the River Wye a few miles north-west of its confluence with the Derwent, date back to well before the Domesday Survey of 1086. Perhaps the church, on rising ground west of the town centre, is the best place to start looking for real antiquities: the tower and spire which dominate the skyline were substantially rebuilt in the nineteenth century, but elsewhere within the building features representing most periods from the twelfth century onwards can be found, all helpfully labelled for the benefit of interested visitors.

Also worth seeking out are the Old House Museum in an early Tudor house in Cunningham Place, the old Town Hall of 1684, and a fine seventeenth-century Market Hall at the junction of Bridge Street with Market Square, converted into a National Park Information Centre. In fact, Bakewell abounds with examples of town architecture from around 1700 for it was then that the Duke of Rutland attempted to establish a spa here to rival Buxton's, 10 miles (16km) across the hills to the north-west and at that time undeveloped.

Unfortunately the project failed! Even Buxton's thermal spring water, bubbling up from deep underground at a constant 28°C (82°F) and recognised as health-promoting since Roman times, required royal patronage, vast amounts of capital, ambitious building programmes and the coming of the railway in 1863 to realise its potential for a spa town. What chance Bakewell, with waters several degrees colder and lacking the lavish expenditure the 5th Duke of Devonshire was to bestow upon his development of Buxton later that century—money acquired from his copper mines on Ecton Hill and which also went into the rebuilding of Chatsworth House. Bakewell's Bath House and Gardens serve as a reminder of its earlier spa aspirations.

And so Bakewell went the way of an agricultural market town in which role it, too, has prospered; its Agricultural Show held each August is one of the biggest in the country. Turning a blind eye to heavy traffic on the A6 which thunders through the town centre (it's hard to see how a by-pass could avoid town, river and enclosing hillsides), the place rewards exploration with a couple of good bookshops, pedestrian shopping arcades and, of course, a chance to buy a Bakewell Pudding!

This local sweet delicacy, much copied and by now a household name in many countries of the world, was created—so the story goes—by accident. Around 1860, a flustered cook at the former White Horse Inn in Matlock Street, instructed to prepare a strawberry tart for some important guests, poured his pastry egg mixture on top of the jam filling by mistake: unexpectedly the dish was declared a success and became a speciality thereafter, growing rapidly in popularity! Two rival establishments claim to have the original recipe—a bakery in Matlock Street and the Original Bakewell Pudding Shop/Restaurant in Bridge Street. Whichever you patronise, Bakewell Puddings make a delicious energy snack for walkers!

From the main car park you cross the multi-parapeted bridge over the Wye north-east of the town centre: built for packhorses in 1664, you will be glad of its 'quoins' or wall recesses which offer pedestrians some protection from modern day traffic. Immediately to your right once across, a delightful riverside walk is populated by a lively community of ducks who show no hesitation in hassling passers-by for tit-bits, though they soon lost interest when I started taking photographs!

The walk actually forks left up Station Road, passing round Castle Hill and onto a minor road on the right which leads you up over the old Midland Railway bridge. Trains have long ceased using this line which once connected Bakewell and Buxton on the London to Manchester route; the trackbed is now a National Park amenity known as the Monsal Trail, its eastern terminus less than a mile to the south-east.

Springtime on the riverside path between Bakewell and Haddon Hall.

A short way past the bridge you branch right on a bridleway across Bakewell Golf Course and up into the northern end of Manners Wood. Just after a zig-zag on a steep part of the scarp slope, you turn right onto a well defined track which rounds a small corner of hillside then contours right along through the woods for over 1½ miles (2.5km). Here and there you dip or climb but by staying on the main track at various intersections you will remain high on the long ridge in a sweep of mature mixed woodland above the Wye valley.

Eventually a right turn is taken, dropping you to the Coombs valley lane which once served as the main connecting route between Rowsley and Bakewell before being superseded by the A6. Left takes you quickly to Three Lanes End, and two subsequent right turns put you on course past Aaron Hole and Shadyside plantations and downhill to Bowling Green Farm. Bridlegates lead on to Haddon Park Farms's access track where you swing sharply round a blocked-off tunnel portal of the old railway and descend to Sheepbridge.

River bank erosion has caused problems south from here but efforts are made to keep the footpath open. With luck you will be able to enjoy a pleasant walk by riverside trees to the A6 about 300m short of Haddon Hall's main entrance. Should the footpath be closed, a rather less enjoyable kilometre or so is involved alongside the A6.

Perched on a limestone slope above the Wye, the grey, battlemented walls and towers of Haddon Hall give the impression—quite correctly—of being a showpiece of English architecture. Unlike nearby Chatsworth, the building does not set out to impress with scale and opulence; it is essentially a superb example of a fortified manor house dating mainly from the sixteenth and seventeenth centuries and has all the appearances of a history book illustration, so carefully has it been maintained and restored.

In fact, the Hall was abandoned by its owners, the Manners family, in the later 1600s when they transferred their seat to Belvoir Castle in Leicestershire. However, the present Duke of Rutland's father (the 9th Duke) devoted a lifetime's work to meticulous restoration, so that what we see today is little changed from the original state. Castle-like battlements atop the walls are a stylistic feature and never saw military action—another factor in the Hall's survival free from major changes due to fashion or damage.

Visits are best accompanied by the guidebook since there is too much detail for inclusion here. I was greatly impressed by the chapel's medieval wall paintings, the kitchen's many original fittings and the bay-windowed Long Gallery, added by Sir John Manners in 1597 by which time building work had virtually come to an end. The flowery, terraced gardens are also well worth seeing and the whole complex is open to the public from Easter to September, excluding Sundays and Mondays.

Steps will need to be retraced to Sheepbridge for a resumption of the return walk to Bakewell. A gate straight ahead leads out to marshy ground in a river bend and on to a copse which is also often squelchy underfoot. If you are unfortunate enough to encounter the river in spate, it may be necessary to divert right to Coombs Lane at the Monsal Trail terminus; otherwise fence stiles form a straightforward path, short-cutting the Wye's snaking meanders and meeting a surfaced lane through Bakewell's showground (which doubles as a Market Day car park). A footbridge over the mill stream and a second over the Wye itself conclude your approach to the town centre which lies a minute or two away.

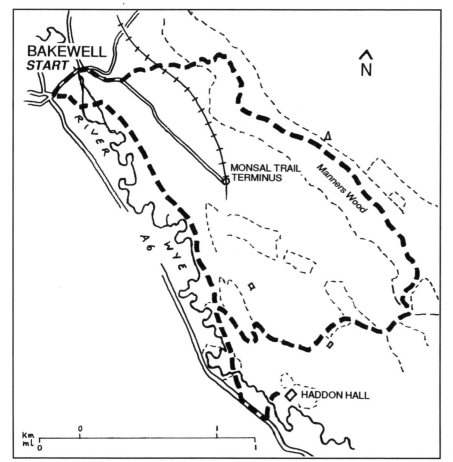

Bakewell market.

Facing page **The Monsal Trail follows the old Bakewell-to-Buxton railway trackbed through dales beside the River Wye—a view from Monsal Head.**

WALK 13: *Dales and Villages from Monsal Head*

Start/Finish: Monsal Head car park. **Access:** Approximately 3 miles (5km) north-west of Bakewell via Ashford-in-the-Water and the B6465. Nearest railway stations—Grindleford and Buxton. **Distance:** 15½ miles (25km)—allow about 6 hours. **Terrain:** Undulating paths, tracks and lanes through dales, by riversides and over the tops. Several refreshment places en route. **Maps:** OS Landranger Sheet 119. Outdoor Leisure White Peak.

Whatever the season, weather, or time of day, the view from Monsal Head must rank as one of the grandest in the National Park. 300ft (91m) below, the River Wye sweeps round in a graceful meandering curve from Cressbrook Mill into Monsal Dale, bounded by the impressive north face of Fin Cop.

Crowning all is the Monsal viaduct, originally built to carry the London-Midland railway line. John Ruskin, the nineteenth century art critic turned social reformer, forthrightly condemned what he saw as the desecration of natural beauty in the pursuit of 'progress'—a standpoint far more attuned to our own age than to his. Certainly, a railway line between Bakewell and Buxton (part of the London to Manchester route) would never today be forced through the picturesque Wye valley. Ironically however, the trackbed is now a National Park trail through the most dramatic countryside and Ruskin's hated viaduct has become a much-admired monument to the Railway Age, protected by the Department of the Environment.

Monsal Head is a busy little focus of activity in the summer months: there are bicycles for hire, meals and drinks on offer and photographs to be taken. But come here in midwinter, except perhaps on a fine Sunday, and you will have it virtually to yourself.

Having savoured the wonderful scenery, you set off left on a path slanting down through woods below a huge landslip called Hob's House, to cross the Wye on a footbridge just beyond the weir. It is a popular spot for birds—water and foliage mean insects—and during the summer you might well see bullfinches, marsh tits, the common sandpiper, redstarts and several of the warbler family. Here and there where the river loops away, the path stands back from its edge, providing clear views of Fin Cop. Dominating the dale's southern bank, this steep and inviting hill bears signs of an Iron Age settlement at its summit but, unfortunately, there is no public access.

As you swing south past clumps of dark bushes and grazing cattle, closer than ever to Fin Cop, a woodland stretch brings you out to the White Lodge car park and picnic site adjacent to the A6 at Lees Bottom. Straight ahead, a clear path strikes up into Deep Dale, taking you through Demon's Dell ('Rock Shelter' on the 1:25,000 map). It appears to have been a burial site for Beaker Folk, those distant ancestors who arrived in Britain from the continent around 1800BC and introduced food vessel pottery. In fact, the path through the ravine is not a definitive right of way—that path is waymarked by posts over open pasture above.

Farther up Deep Dale the ambience grows

much less intimate. Crunching through virgin snow one February Sunday, my companion and I could see countless animal and bird tracks weaving hither and thither over the frozen surface—a graphic reminder that while we toast ourselves in front of fires and consume packaged food, wild creatures are constantly engaged in the struggle to eat and find shelter. That same day, out on the plateau, snow had drifted into unbelievably complex forms—hollowed, fluted, corkscrewed and waved—so that you walked through a landscape of endlessly changing white sculptures.

Emerging from the dale, you turn right up a lane past Over Wheal Farm and left at the little crossroads beyond. For a time, Taddington village is lost from sight behind rising ground, but after turning right along a B road you reach a small saddle on Taddington Moor and fork right down to the long main street.

Numerous springs rising in this part of the White Peak probably account for Taddington's siting. It is a large village, gently uphill from east to west, and although its dwellings are modest in scale and style, its church is a rather imposing structure set on the highest ground. Six hundred years ago, the wool and lead

trades were in full swing and the prosperity they generated allowed the building or reconstruction of some splendid churches. Far more grandiose than Taddington's is that at nearby Tideswell, built almost exclusively in the Decorated style and a cathedral in everything but name.

Mercifully, the busy A6 which must have once been the bane of Taddington's life is now swept along to the north as a modern by-pass. Tasteful cottage conversions underscore how such a development can radically enhance a village's desirability for prospective home owners and holidaymakers. There is a Post Office-cum-general store opposite St. Michael's Church, also a cafe and an hotel alongside the A6 to the west.

Before reaching the churchyard, you take a lane towards Chapel Farm which forks right across small enclosure fields. By-pass traffic is fast and furious and rudely interrupts the pace of walking, so it is worth waiting for a safe lull in which to scurry across! Still on the field track, you pass a sharp left junction but off the next bend keep straight ahead, now on a footpath linking wall stiles.

The down-and-up over High Dale is quite

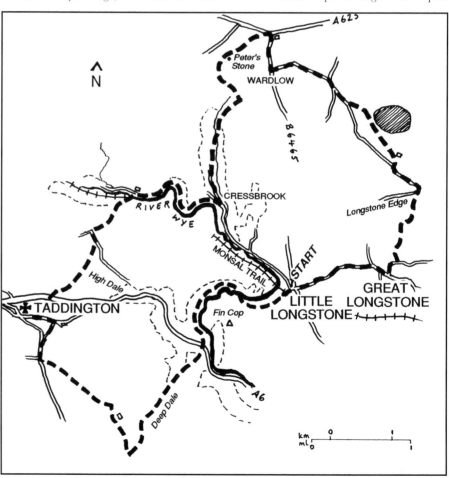

steep and can be slippery in rain or frost. At the top of the tiny side valley opposite, you turn left onto a by-road and, 100m later, turn right alongside a wall. Keeping in the same general direction (ie north-east), you will soon begin a more sustained descent over scrubby pasture into the deeply incised Wye valley. Crossing a bridge spanning the Monsal Trail trackbed and another over the Wye, you reach the Litton Mill complex.

The mile or so of sinuous river bed separating Litton and Cressbrook mills is known, cheerily, as Water-cum-Jolly. At the beginning of the nineteenth century, these two mills were differentiated in another, far less frivolous way which a little digression will serve to explain.

Richard Arkwright, the Industrial Revolution's great pioneer of water powered machinery, is best known in a Peak District context for his textile mills at Cromford where, aided by the rushing Derwent, cottage industry was transformed to factory-scale production. However, he also created other mills in the Peak, including the original one at Cressbrook, some of which have been restored and are in use by modern industrial enterprises. Other men followed Arkwright's lead, using water power to grind corn, crush mineral ores and pulp rags for paper-making, as well as to spin and weave textiles.

Now while Arkwright's pauper apprentices at Cressbrook were well cared for by the standards then prevailing—even educated after a fashion—those employed by a certain Ellis Needham at Litton Mill were subjected to appalling cruelty and degradation, as 'A Memoir of Robert Blincoe', published in 1828, shockingly reveals. Changes in factory law were long overdue and by no means all mill owners were benevolently disposed towards their workforce.

Litton and Cressbrook tunnels on the Monsal Trail are both closed, so forward progress is made along a broad concessionary track on the Wye's north bank past rock outcrops and reed beds to Cressbrook Mill. If circumstances dictate a curtailment of the walk here, you could cross the Cressbrook mill race and weir footbridge, climbing steps to a newish path leading up to the Monsal Trail. Once over the viaduct at Monsal Head, access to the road above is clearly waymarked.

The second half of this walk has a rather different character—more open and with enticing views north to where White Peak and Dark Peak merge. But first there is a dale of distinction to ascend, in my opinion quite the most beautiful of the Wye's tributaries. Facing north at Cressbrook Mill (recently in process of renovation and well worth admiring), you branch right on the narrow lane up Cressbrook Dale.

Peter's Stone.

Clothed in native woodland throughout its lower reaches, it is a haven for many species of flora and fauna and contains a Nature Reserve.

A right fork is taken to pass Ravensdale Cottages, dominated by a rock-climbers' crag of the same name (Raven's Buttress on maps) whereafter you cross a footbridge and mount scrubby hillside to an exhilarating high-level path providing superb views of the upper dale snaking on ahead. No right of way exists at the same height all the way up so one is obliged to follow the well defined path angling downhill to the valley bottom wall.

In winter a stream often shares the confines of upper Cressbrook Dale with you and, as a result, the going can be very marshy. Soon Peter's Stone looms high on the right bank. It appears curiously displaced and has, in fact, slumped to its present position over thousands of years thanks to the lubricating action of underlying soft green clay. Its profile—hence its name—is said to resemble that of St. Peter's Basilica in Rome.

Emerging at a gate by farm buildings, and ignoring for a moment the busy A623 at your feet, there is a vivid sense of having surfaced, as it were, into a different kind of countryside. Gone are the intimacies of dale and riverside, to be replaced by open prospects towards the transition from limestone to millstone grit.

A short stroll south up the B6465 and you turn left on a cross-country course, mostly on little used lanes. A right turn at the next junction is quickly followed by a fork left, taking you uphill in the direction of Longstone Edge on a by-road you could easily stay with if it takes your fancy. However, if tarmac and traffic are anathema—and they usually are to walkers—branch off left on the next track. It disappears into a lake of uncertain depth and content which at my last visit was prettified by pastel hues of ice, but you can cut up across a field to the right, through Longstone Moor Farm and regain the by-road just short of Longstone Edge itself.

In recent years, quiet uplands between

Eyam and Great Longstone have suffered brutal disembowelment from the extraction of fluorspar, a valuable flux employed in steel making. The mines and opencast workings around High Rake on Longstone Edge, with their complements of heavy machinery and lorries, have created an unsightly environment. Mud, dust and periodic earth-shaking explosions conspire to deter walkers, though on detailed investigation it is possible to make a circular route along High Rake to Sallet Hole Mine and back via Deep Rake—a grimly fascinating extension to this otherwise tranquil itinerary!

From the hairpin road bend on Longstone Edge you follow a fence beneath a bank of spoil for a few metres before crossing it at a stile and descending to the right of an eroded channel. Views south are panoramic and may well distract you from route-finding! The pathway is none too clear on the ground at first as it drops down the bushy scarp slope, but it rapidly improves, crosses pasture and enters a dry valley. Further down you will reach a lane above Great Longstone's church, turning right to the village centre.

The walk's final mile lies west along the minor road, past shop and pub and on through Little Longstone. Both villages are endowed with pretty stone houses, some quite old, and after so much countryside it is a delight to gaze upon the cosy façades of buildings and carefully tended gardens.

Below left: **Snowdrifts in Deep Dale.**

Below: **St. Michael's Church is set on Taddington's highest ground.**
Bottom: **Winter in upper Cressbrook Dale.**

Facing page: **The imposing façade of Chatsworth House.**

Walk 14: *Chatsworth Park*

Start/Finish: Baslow car park. **Access:** Baslow lies on the A619, 8 miles (13km) west of Chesterfield. Nearest railway station—Grindleford. **Distance:** 8 miles (13km)—allow 4 hours plus time for the formal gardens and interior. **Terrain:** Well established footpaths and tracks over hilly, semi-natural parkland. **Maps:** OS Landranger Sheet 119. Outdoor Leisure White Peak.

Chatsworth's stately home and landscaped parkland deserve more than a cursory visit. Whilst the splendours of the interior fall outside the remit of a book about walking, an exploration of the grounds makes a very fine outing indeed. The whole walk is steeped in history and further reading would undoubtedly enrich your appreciation of Chatsworth's origins, occupants and architectural development.

Surroundings on this hike cannot lay claim to being 'wild', yet carefully maintained tracks and pathways find their counterpoint in woods and rough pastureland with all the hilly spaciousness of open country. The landscape, of course, is not a 'natural' one, having been profoundly transformed by a succession of ducal families. In the 1760s, most of the formal gardens were modified by the famous Capability Brown whose grand designs entailed changing the course of the River Derwent and taming this moorland valley with plantations and expansive deer park grassland.

The first Chatsworth House was put up by Sir William and Lady Cavendish (Bess of Hardwick) in the 1550's but was to suffer an abortive attempt by the 4th Earl to make drastic alterations in the Classical style. Ultimately, William Cavendish, who had become the 1st Duke of Devonshire in 1694, remodelled the house to his own plans, enlisting the advice of William Talman and Thomas Archer, both architects of the English Baroque. Apart from the addition of a north wing by the 6th Duke in 1820 which included a new library, sculpture gallery and theatre, the building that confronts us today is fundamentally little changed from its eighteenth century form.

Chatsworth is a very large mansion—more of a community really if you include the estate village of Edensor—and its size is enhanced by first views across great sweeps of elegant hillside. The superb rock gardens, pinetum and arboretum were created by Sir Joseph Paxton, head estate gardener from 1826, and rare plants were brought in from far-flung lands to stock the glasshouses. Paxton, more than a gardener, was astute in business, a writer of some talent and would become architect of London's Crystal Palace. East of the house, water cascades from jets on the hillside, splashing over terraced steps before vanishing underground, but it is the Emperor Fountain that steals the show—a 290ft (90m) plume claiming, when it was installed, to be the highest of its kind in the world!

Although you can drive through the western part of the estate on the B6012 between Baslow and Beeley, other roads within the park—like the house itself—are only open seasonally. However, most of what there is to see of the grounds is accessible to walkers who, in any case, will always enjoy the most favourable perspectives.

A start from Baslow is easy to arrange and holds the promise of refreshments at the end of the walk should the cafe at Chatsworth be closed. From the car park a fenced tracks leads clearly to high metal gates at the estate perimeter. You now take a south-east course uphill over tree-dotted deer park, crossing the main access road and, higher up, a track, to reach a bank and stile. Ahead the way climbs quite steeply up the wooded scarp (against which the entire Chatsworth complex is ranged), passes a disused quarry and emerges onto a metalled lane.

Turning right along a track you will catch a glimpse of the Hunting Tower down a ride in Stand Wood; an elaborate lookout, or 'gazebo', it dates from the mid-sixteenth century when Chatsworth first became established. The track winds round to cross the Emperor Stream at its entry into Emperor Lake then swings right along the west shore of Swiss Lake. Veering right again through a gate/stile, then left and crossing a metalled lane from Park Farm, you turn left and leave Stand Wood for the edge-top path above Beeley. After only 150m or so the way forks right down through bracken to a door and stile and the minor road at Beeley Hilltop Farm, continuing downhill to Beeley Lodge and the B6012.

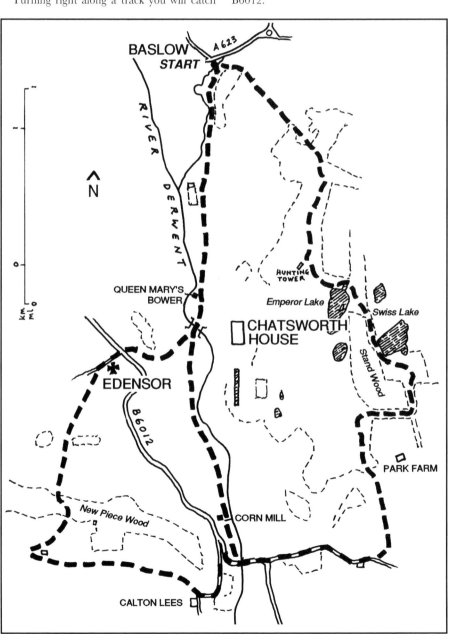

One Arch Bridge spanning the River Derwent represents the work of James Paine who also built Chatsworth Bridge, facing the house itself, and the stable block to the north. Paine replaced the original east-west estate road with the present north-south one which fits the lie of the land much more sympathetically.

A stile immediately on your right gives access to a meadow path beside the river. Ahead stands the Old Corn Mill, put up around 1760 in a style compatible with the statue mansion and thus somewhat removed from the vernacular stereotype. Nonetheless, a working mill it was—grinding corn until 1950—and a splendid little architectural curiosity it has remained since, though gale damage in the early 1960s rendered it a virtual ruin. At my last visit, a lone milestone lay against a wall, mute testimony to a once busy scene.

If a direct return to Baslow is required, you simply carry on due north alongside the Derwent, crossing Chatsworth bridge to Queen Mary's Bower and regaining the estate gates not far from the car park—a total distance of 2 miles (3.2km). However, I can recommend the following loop as well worth taking, for no tour of Chatsworth is complete without visiting Edensor.

From Calton Lees car park, you walk south along the road towards Calton Lees Farm but leave it at an acute bend for a valley track on the right. This leads up beneath Lees Wood to Calton Houses. Zig-zagging up to a gate, you walk between the dwellings where a second stile gives out to a track climbing over pasture. A footpath crossing at right-angles further up-slope connects Russian Cottage (tucked up in the field corner and named after the 6th Duke's friendship with the Czar) with Bakewell town, but the cottage itself is private.

New Piece Wood straddles a ridge and once you have reached its crest it is downhill all the way to Edensor. A Chatsworth Park signboard announces your emergence into acres of rough parkland grazed by fallow deer and pheasant.

Remote, here, from the hubbub created by car and coach-borne sightseers who arrive in prodigious numbers during the holiday season, you do gain space and time in which to ponder how the great Whig and Protestant landowners of the seventeenth century became Britain's true masters. Chatsworth, Castle Howard and Blenheim Palace are, indeed, extravagant monuments to those grandees who survived the long war years with France and put the Hanoverians on the throne.

Spared the destruction of war and revolution, British houses and castles reflect a relative stability and continuity in the social order. Modified or adapted over the centuries but encapsulating the past in the quality of building materials and accumulated treasures, these eminent palaces and estates provide us common mortals with a glimpse of untold wealth and privilege. Times change, and as the elements take their toll of masonry and timber, and as the cost of labour soars, many a stately home has opted to admit visits by a curious public rather than dispose of what amounts to part of our national heritage.

The walk resumes down towards two plantations. By steering to the right of the circular one (Maud's Plantation), you will come upon a waymark post, whereafter the spire of Edensor's church is aimed for directly. With Chatsworth House visible in the background and Edensor's rooftops coming into view, you swing left of the churchyard and find a metal gate with railings above a flight of stone steps leading to the village street.

Edensor (pronounced 'Ensor') was formerly sited between the road and the Derwent but was relocated lock, stock and barrel by the 6th Duke of Devonshire between 1838 and 1842; the old village was demolished so as not to spoil the immediate environs of Chatsworth House. Sir Joseph Paxton planned the new village layout and designed some of its houses, others being the work of J.C. Robertson.

Edensor strikes you as a sedate, well ordered place, more homogeneous with its uniform blue paintwork and houses of similar date than a 'normal' village community. St. Peter's Church, built by Sir Gilbert Scott and consecrated in 1866, dominates all. In its churchyard, as you would expect, are buried the former Dukes of Devonshire and their families, but it may come as a surprise to find the grave of Kathleen Kennedy, daughter of U.S. Ambassador Joseph Kennedy and sister of none other than the late John F. Kennedy, President of the United States.

Over the B6012, a surfaced pathway rises through scattered trees and dips gently to Chatsworth Bridge, one of two built by James Paine and a perfect foreground for classic views of Chatsworth House. If desired, the formal gardens and tours of the splendid interior are best reached from this point, nearing the end of the walk.

Just north of a kissing gate off the road will be found Queen Mary's Bower. Mary Queen of Scots was held prisoner at Chatsworth by Bess of Hardwick's fourth husband, the Earl of Shrewsbury, in the late 1500s and would 'take the air' in this curious, rather grandiose summer house. In utter contrast, I was glad to shelter beneath its arch from torrential, freezing rain one winter's day in an attempt to rekindle some vestige of body warmth with a flask of lukewarm coffee and soggy sandwiches!

Onwards, the path flanks a cricket ground and the estate nursery, finally running alongside Bar Brook, a minor tributary of the Derwent, to the metal boundary gates. It is time to take a last backwards look at the broad sweep of Chatsworth's semi-natural landscape, for there is nothing else like it in the National Park. The fleshpots of Baslow beckon and will transport you, rudely perhaps, back to the realities of hectic twentieth century life!

St. Peter's Church Edensor, seen from Chatsworth's parklands.

Walk 15: *The Monsal Trail and Chee Dale*

Start/Finish: Car park, former Miller's Dale station. **Access:** Miller's Dale lies on the B6049 between Tideswell and the A6 due east of Buxton.
Distance: 5½ miles (9km)—allow about 3½ hours. **Terrain:** Railway trackbed, tortuous riverside path, field tracks and country lanes. **Maps:** OS Landranger Sheet 119. Outdoor Leisure White Peak.

If the landscapes of the White Peak's central plateau seem gentle and softly rolling like a Mozart sonata, then Chee Dale is pure Wagner! Westwards from Ashford-in-the-Water, the River Wye has carved a sinuous course in the limestone bedrock through Monsal Dale, Water-cum-Jolly Dale, Litton Dale and Ashwood Dale. Roads show you little of this geological drama—one of the few remaining 'wild' places in Peakland—and it is only those venturing forth on foot who will discover such secret wonders of nature.

All is not unsullied by the hand of man, however, though the intrusion occurred over a century ago. With the Railway Age already well in ascendancy, the London-Midland line between St. Pancras and Manchester was completed in the 1860s. It ran through this delectable rocky valley (some of the most difficult country imaginable for a railway) and involved massive environmental disruption. Lengthy tunnels had to be blasted through obstructing hillsides, while thousands of tons of shale were dumped in the river gorge.

John Ruskin, that great romantic and conservationist, was moved to declare bitterly that, '. . . The valley is gone and the Gods with it, and now every fool in Buxton can be at Bakewell in half an hour and every fool in Bakewell at Buxton; which you think a lucrative process of exchange—you Fools everywhere . . .' Scathing words, embodying the sentiment that the end does not always justify the means, that the advantages of quicker travel were outweighed by the desecration of outstanding natural beauty. It is a sentiment we are slowly returning to, though in those pre-conservation days there was little call for our industrious forefathers to consider the environmental consequences of their actions.

The railway lasted a hundred years. In 1981, the Peak Park Board finally reached agreement with British Rail to open the trackbed for leisure use by the public and the Monsal Trail was born, leading walkers past superb limestone scenery from Monsal Head to Wye Dale. In the longer term it is, indeed, an ill wind . . .

But first, a word of caution: west of Miller's Dale car park, an unsafe tunnel has been sealed off, forcing you to enter the Chee Dale gorge around Chee Tor. Since this forms the walk's scenic climax, no-one is complaining, but the footpath just beyond Chee Tor takes to a line of stepping stones where the Wye runs

between sheer rock walls. Should river levels be high, you may be unable to pass without a wetting and will need to retrace your steps. If this is the case, why not try an alternative walk north through Wormhill to Peter Dale and a return via Monk's Dale Nature Reserve? Distances are very similar.

The tiny community of Miller's Dale huddles uncomfortably beneath the old London-Midland station near an impressive viaduct. During the last century it was home to workers in local industries which sprang up after the railway had arrived, but they have long since disappeared. Today, the old station buildings and yard have been converted into a car park and toilets, the site's size betraying its former importance as a junction station. The main line to Manchester swung northwest up Great Rocks Dale (and is still in use by lime quarries there), while the Buxton branch line continued westwards, shadowing the River Wye.

You set off along the cinder trackbed past old platforms and soon reach disused limekilns on the right. The limeworks themselves were demolished by explosives in 1971 but the four stone limekilns, dating from 1878, are safe to visit and are reached by a clear, rising path. A short distance ahead, the onward trackbed is impassable due to a sealed tunnel, so the path ducks down steps into the wooded bowels of Chee Dale.

Immediately you are close beside the River Wye, its waters tumbling over shallow weirs. Increasingly rocky, the path climbs up around the marshy, gurgling resurgence of Wormhill Springs at the base of Flag Dale, crossing two footbridges in the process and leading you into

the vegetated depths of an imposing gorge.

Chee Tor never fails to impress. Its 300ft (91m) wall of vertical limestone provides some of the most challenging rock climbs in the National Park and you may be forgiven for taking a prolonged break here to watch the action! Fifty acres around you are managed as a Nature Reserve by the Derbyshire Naturalists' Trust.

Less hazardous than climbing, certainly, but demanding care nonetheless, especially in wet weather, the path utilises natural ledges and steps above the river bed. Rather sinister overhangs of black, dripping rock push out above your head and soon what riverbank there was has given out altogether. A total of about 40 stepping stones stretch ahead under the cliff—simplicity itself in good conditions but ranging from mildly hazardous to impassable (unless you accept getting wet!) when the river is in spate.

Difficulties are soon behind you and at a footbridge near another railway masonry arch, a concessionary footpath strikes up left onto the Monsal Trail at the western portal of the sealed tunnel. Despite a grant by British Rail of £154,000 towards the cost of repairs, the Peak Park Board have yet to finalise work in the Trail. The line only ceased operation in 1968 and the original coarse gravel ballast now encountered will, presumably, be removed one day; in the meantime it is not the easiest of surfaces to walk upon!

Two shorter tunnels are passed through and there is a slight opening out of the dale. To the left of the trackbed where it crosses a bridge over the Wye soars Plum Buttress, another limestone crag of great interest to clim-

Facing page: **West of Miller's Dale the path dives into the wooded bowels of Chee Dale beside the River Wye.**

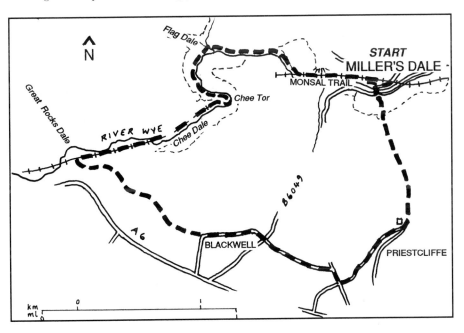

bers. While you crunch along, you might, as I have done, reflect on public attitudes prevailing in the mid-nineteenth century which allowed a railway to be driven through this remarkably beautiful valley. It may, of course, have been a lack of public awareness—long before mass communication brought issues to a wider audience—that gave industrialists free rein in their pursuit of profit.

Half a mile further on, just after walking beneath a bridge, you cross a wall stile and climb a broad, grassy track up a minor side valley. In 200m or so, a narrow path on the left zig-zags very steeply up the daleside, meets another trod and breaks through onto the farmland plateau.

Here is a viewpoint 'par excellence' and one to savour if you have the time, for it signals your departure from Chee Dale. The Monsal Trail itself reaches its terminus half a mile to the west at Wye Dale car park. On the opposite bank of the Wye, the old main line trackbed can be seen snaking into Great Rocks Dale—a tributary valley—to join a mineral line from the huge Tunstead Quarry complex.

Up there, largely unseen from this angle, all thoughts of natural beauty can be forgotten. This is Europe's largest producer of limestone, the exceptional purity of which guarantees the continuing expansion of quarry workings well into the next century. Flanked by railway lines directly below you across the River Wye are Blackwell Mill Cottages, put up to house railway workers and their families and once served by a tiny Halt; Blackwell Mill itself has gone.

You next proceed east alongside a wall, over a stile up across fields to enter a delightful walled green lane; it will bring you out past a small caravan and camping site at Blackwell hamlet. Beyond Blackwell Hall's drive and the B6049 (which makes a beeline for Miller's Dale down Blackwell Dale), country lanes are followed through Priestcliffe Ditch and left to Priestcliffe. Up to your right are signs of Celtic or early Saxon stepped lynchets—a form of early terraced cultivation on steep hillside.

You head now for Lydgate Farm and follow a field track north off the road bend. At its first corner leftwards, after a distance of about 500m, a footpath carries straight ahead downslope through stiles, enters steep woods at the western edge of a large disused limeworks and reaches Miller's Dale just above the road bridge. Throughout the descent there are wide views of the surrounding limestone uplands.

A short, steep pull up the road and under the railway bridge brings you back to the car park, but don't overlook the friendly little cafe opposite which welcomes hikers with a range of drinks and snacks!

Above and below: **Rock ledges and overhanging walls characterise the path as it penetrates the depths of Chee Dale.**

Wellington's Monument

Walk 16: *The South-Eastern Gritstone Edges*

Start/Finish: Robin Hood car park. **Access:** Off the A619, 2 miles (3km) east of Baslow. Nearest railway stations—Grindleford, Dore & Totley, and Chesterfield. **Distance:** 11 miles (17.5km). **Terrain:** Undulating rocky paths above gritstone edges, interspersed with a little rough moorland. **Maps:** OS Landranger Sheet 119. Outdoor Leisure White Peak.

Running south to north for a distance of almost 15 miles (24km) in the east of the National Park is a succession of high gritstone edges. Almost continuous, they form a gigantic 'step' at which sombre moorland gives way to the shale valley of the Derwent and the gentler, pastoral landscapes beyond.

Laid down by river deltas from the Carboniferous Age which once covered the White Peak, the cap of millstone grit has been eroded away to form the distinctive edge scenery we know today. Seen from afar, these ramparts of bare rock thrust against the sky are compelling enough; but close to, when intricacies of form and texture can be fully perceived, they become a focus of magnetic fascination.

The abrasive nature of Peakland grit not only gave rise to a once flourishing millstone industry—abandoned stones still lie below the rock faces from which they were hewn—but was responsible in large part for the birth of rock climbing in this country around the turn of the century.

Many of Britain's finest climbers cut their teeth on the crags of Stanage, Curbar and Froggatt edges before turning their attention to the Alps and the Himalayas. During the 1950s and 60s, men like Joe Brown, the late Don Whillans and other well known characters—often from the nearby conurbations of Manchester and Sheffield—pioneered extreme routes on this firm, eminently climbable rock.

Their height may be modest—up to 60ft (18m) on Stanage Edge—but the crags present climbers with a vast range of problems and challenges. Whatever the weather, you will almost certainly share this outing with those who choose a more intimate encounter with this world of vertical rock: climbing here is an institution!

Where the lines of cliff are breached by a hiatus or a temporary easing of angle, nonclimbers may scramble about to their heart's content, but for walkers the great joy of these edges are the broad and airy paths which thread along the tops. You are not always on the rocky lip itself (though you can often divert to it), but there is a marvellous sense of elevation and views can be stunningly beautiful.

It all starts at the car park beside the Eric Byne Memorial campsite near the Robin Hood pub just off the A619 east of Baslow. A short way up the B6050, a ladder stile on the left leads you along by a wall to a path fork. In fact, either way will get you to grips with the bouldery, birch-clad slopes leading to Birchen Edge, followed by an easy scramble to the top.

Nelson's Monument—not the most imposing of obelisks—was erected in 1810 by a John Brightman from Baslow; the inscription '1865'

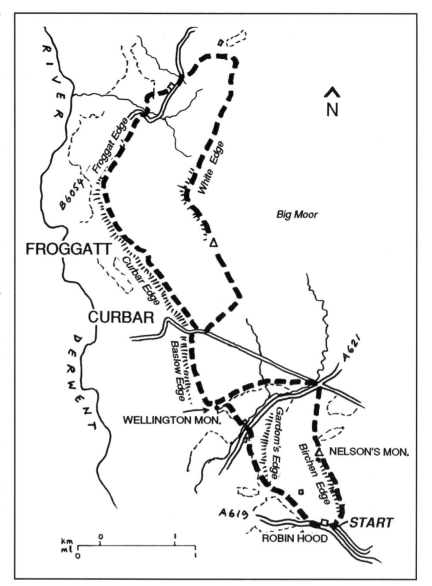

is merely old fashioned graffiti! Nearby are rocky prows named after three of Nelson's ships—the *Victory*, *Defiant* and *Royal Soverin*. Even below the OS pillar (1017ft—310m) the gritstone slabs reach no great stature, but in clear weather this is a fine viewpoint.

Descending northwards, the path crosses persistently boggy ground right on the perimeter of Access Land, though there is no indication of this; down at the A621 crossroads, however, by the ladder stile, there is indeed an 'Open Country' notice. You walk up the road opposite for about 200m where a gate on the left and another 'Open County' sign lead you onto a good track—the old Chesterfield Road—above the wooded Bar Brook valley.

Wellington's Monument, a solid cross set on a rock base, commands a magnificent view

back to Nelson's Monument and Gardom's Edge, a lower tier of gritstone unseen from Birchen Edge. The monument was put up by Dr. E. M. Wrench in 1866 and bears Wellington's dates—1769 to 1852.

By continuing down to the left you would soon reach Baslow village—gateway to the Chatsworth estate—and should worsening weather indicate a retreat from the tops, there are several possible walking routes midway between the edges and the Derwent valley.

North-west from Wellington's Monument our onward course tracks some distance back from Baslow Edge itself, but you can thread your way along the rock-bound rim by detouring left. In days past, the young bloods of Baslow had to scale the Eagle Stone, to the right of the path, to prove their readiness for marriage! Well walked, the path continues north to Curbar Gap, a superb vantage point over to the moors around Eyam and Stoney Middleton, as well as ahead to the buttresses and slabs of Curbar Edge. It is another spot where the crags relent, allowing a road to pass through connecting Derwent valley settlements with Sheffield. Needless to say, village properties a mere half-hour's drive from the city and situated in such delectable countryside are highly desirable to commuters!

A car park has been established by the National Park authorities at Curbar Gap, providing ready access to edge walks in both directions. Beyond a kissing gate, progress is made along rugged Curbar Edge. The path, rising and falling in rocky steps, is reminiscent of many other locations in Britain where you walk over the very bones of the earth. I once trudged and splashed along here in driving rain and zero visibility and remember thinking that

(rock types apart) it could have been the Cornwall coast path or somewhere in Snowdonia.

But in good conditions this is a promenade to savour. If you fancy a leisurely pace, why not explore the edge itself where the land falls

Looking ahead towards Curbar Edge from Baslow Edge.

away into a complexity of walls and bays, ledges and cracks and on which—little doubt—rock climbers will be engaged in a game of agility, nerve, balance and grip.

After the path swings right and loses height before returning to the edge, you are above Bee Wood and Froggatt village, at the undefined conjunction between Curbar Edge and Froggatt Edge. To the east stretches Big Moor and the unmistakeable spine of another, higher, bastion of millstone grit—White Edge—trodden by the return leg of this itinerary.

Moorland on your right hand side, dotted with curious boulders, cairns and, soon to be encountered, a stone circle, seems charged with a kind of ancient mystery, though I have no real evidence to support this impression. You eventually reach a kissing gate and cross a stream draining Stoke Flat; to the left is the top of Brookside Buttress, just one of a plethora of climbing routes at all grades on the

Curbar/Froggatt Edge which, along with Stanage Edge further north, is very highly regarded by the climbing fraternity.

Continuing north, the popular track increasingly loses contact with the scarp which, in any case, becomes fragmented in the birch woods above the rising B6054. Nevertheless, you can still locate it here and there and, through a veil of trees, admire views out across Grindleford to the foot of Eyam Moor.

A gate gives onto the busy B6054 which has to be crossed in order to descend and ford the little valley bottom stream. You climb to a fence stile and turn right past the National Trust car park, taking a path up through two fields to the Grouse Inn. Approximately 250m up the road, a track strikes off to the right over rough hillside and, keeping south of White Edge Lodge and a small plantation, rises through a fence at a line of boulders onto White Edge Moor. You can now pick up a

trod running south and passing through a wall towards the main gritstone outcrop of White Edge, pock marked from target practice during World War II and called the Bullet Stones.

More broken and vegetated than the edges below, White Edge dips gently to a stream then, at a shallow, curving corner, regains a little height. Well defined throughout, the path over heathery ground takes you past an OS pillar at 1197ft (365m) where the rocks finally peter out and you are heading downhill towards an enclosure wall. Swinging right at its corner, the way crosses Sandyford Brook on a wooden footbridge and arrives at Curbar Gap car park.

As a rule, I prefer not to tread ground already covered on the outward stage of a circular walk, but in this case the 1km along Baslow Edge is unavoidable. Once at Wellington's Monument, you double back beneath the scarp alongside a wall. Lower down Jack Flat the going gets decidedly squelchy, but after a stile you flank a garden, cross Bar Brook on an old packhorse bridge and get to the other side of the A621!

Beyond Cupola Cottage, a clear path angles uphill in and out of trees below Gardom's Edge, with its conspicuous cairns known as The Three Men. Not far from Moorside Farm you pass over a circular bank (origin unknown!) and reach a stile beside the busy A619 Chesterfield road. You have only to stride up the pavement for 250m to find the Robin Hood pub and the adjacent car park from which you set out.

Walk 17: *Villages and Moors around Eyam*

Start/Finish: Hawkhill car park, Eyam. **Access:** Eyam lies just north of the A623 west of Stoney Middleton on the Chesterfield to Manchester via Chapel-en-le-Frith road. Nearest railway station—Grindleford. **Distance:** 12 miles (19km)—allow 6 hours plus time in Eyam. **Terrain:** Field, moor and riverside paths, the latter often muddy. A few steep gradients. **Maps:** OS Landranger Sheets 110 and 119. Outdoor Leisure White Peak and Dark Peak.

Superb viewpoints, interesting old villages and houses and a wide variety of landscapes there certainly are on this exhilarating walk, yet for visitors with a love of history and a vivid imagination, Eyam (pronounced 'Eem') itself will induce immense fascination. In addition to time spent walking, it is advisable to allow at least an hour in which to absorb the sights and associations of this famous 'Plague Village'.

Eyam's origins date back to Roman times, its early Saxon name—Aiune—meaning 'settlement by the water'. Indeed, an abundance of fresh water encouraged the village's early growth, as it did in many Peakland locations, but it was lead mining that brought real prosperity. Ironically, as mines penetrated ever deeper underground, water became the enemy, flooding workings and ultimately presenting insurmountable technical problems so that by the end of the nineteenth century the industry had virtually disappeared.

Periodic outbreaks of bubonic plague had ravaged Britain for 300 years before London's historic epidemic in 1665 which, as every schoolchild knows, was followed a year later by the Great Fire. Eyam's own story also begins in 1665 when a travelling tailor, George Viccars, took lodgings with Mary Cooper, widow of a lead miner. A box of cloth was subsequently delivered from London in late August and its contents, found to be damp, were laid out to dry by Viccars who fell ill shortly afterwards.

It is generally believed that rat fleas infected with the plague bacillus bit Viccars and were released into the community, thus setting in train a sequence of events that have gone down in history as both poignantly tragic and a testimony to the fortitude of the human spirit. Bubonic plague strikes quickly and within less than a week Viccars was dead. In mid-September Mary Cooper's son, Edward, died, followed shortly by deaths in adjacent houses.

And so the disease spread, relenting during the colder winter months but reasserting itself with renewed vigour the next summer when it reached its peak. More residents fled in those first dreadful months than later, but it must be remembered that Eyam was an isolated village and that few could abandon homes and livelihoods: in any case, who would welcome them once their reasons for leaving were revealed?

In times long before the advent of medical science, the plague was seen as Divine retribution, the consequences of collective sin. Today it is hard to imagine the unspeakable terror endured by Eyam villagers as, family by family, they were struck down by an apparently random killer. Of cures there were none—herbs, charms and poultices barely

Plague Cottage, home of widow Mary Cooper where Eyam's tragic epidemic of Bubonic plague is thought to have started.

Right: **Descending into the dramatic little valley of Bretton Brook; Abney Grange Farm top right.**

Below: **A tapestry of meadows and drystone walls near Foolow.**

73

alleviated the symptoms let alone tackled the cause.

Only gradually was sense made of the disease's course. Clothing and domestic animals were widely believed to be carriers but slaughter of the latter simply allowed rats—true villains of the piece—to breed unhindered. A few lucky souls contracted a mild bout and developed natural immunity, but by August 1666 about half the population of Eyam—some 200 people—had perished.

Village priests Thomas Stanley and young William Mompesson, though widely different in ages and religious views, decided on a course of action which would result in Eyam earning a prominent place in the recorded history of rural England. At a public meeting it was decided to stop churchyard burials (thereafter people buried their own dead with maximum haste); to hold services in the open air, thus reducing close personal contact; and—most significantly of all—to impose a 'cordon sanitaire' around the village to prevent further spread of the disease.

Deeply held Christian convictions about the virtues of self sacrifice ensured the quarantine's success. Food and other supplies, furnished by the Duke of Devonshire who lived at nearby Chatsworth House, were deposited at special points and paid for by coins left under running water, as at Mompesson's Well, or in holes filled with vinegar.

Quite suddenly, after 14 months and 260 fatalities, it was all over. Indeed, bubonic plague throughout Europe seems to have all but disappeared by 1700, probably owing to improved sanitation and the decline of the black rat. The disease still exists and remains dangerous, but there are modern drugs to treat it with. (The whole story in greater detail can be gleaned from 'Eyam Plague', an informative booklet written and published by John G. Clifford and available from bookshops in the Peak District.)

There is a village trail linking all the plague sites, but even without its benefit you can wander past the old cottages and ponder the wall plaques which identify them. I recommend a visit to St. Lawrence's Church, with its unusual eighteenth-century sundial, for here in the churchyard are a splendidly preserved Saxon cross and the tomb of Mompesson's wife, Katherine, whom he buried on 25th August 1666. Inside the church are Saxon and Norman fonts, some interesting medieval wall paintings, Mompesson's chair and a book recording the names and dates of plague victims. Close by the church stands the very cottage where George Viccars received his fateful delivery of cloth.

The walk itself begins south from the Hawk hill car park, past seventeenth-century Eyam Hall and the old village stocks, where a right turn takes you up through a council estate, over two lanes and on across fields towards Foolow. Wall stiles ensure you keep to the correct line—there are over 20 of them in all—and once you have crossed diminutive Linen Dale you follow the road for the last 250m into Foolow. In spring and summer this is a delightful stretch, ankle deep in flowery meadows and accompanied all the way by a tapestry of drystone walls and views north to Eyam Edge.

Foolow, seductively arranged around an unusually expansive green with its 'mere' (pond), fourteenth-century cross and the village bullring set in a large boulder, has become a prime target for occupation by commuters. Farm buildings—even the eighteenth-century Spread Eagle pub—are now tastefully converted and highly desirable properties in a quintessentially rural setting within easy reach of Sheffield. Nonetheless, Foolow exudes charm and everywhere you look are little cameos of village picturesqueness. Of five pubs, only the Bull's Head has survived, reflecting the disappearance of thirst-provoking work such as lead mining and farm labouring and the steady trend away from traditional village life.

You turn right opposite the cross and stride out along the Bretton road for about 500m. Where the road bends right and begins to climb, you follow a sequence of stiles across rising fields which contain shaft heads from the old lead mines. This short section culminates in a stiff pull up through scrubby vegetation to the summit of Hucklow Edge. Further west the edge curves north as a notable scarp, atop which the Lancashire and Derbyshire Gliding Club have their headquarters at Camphill.

The valley of Bretton Brook is a surprisingly deep and dramatic one, its sides landslipped and bush-speckled. Taking it by the throat, the walk dives straight down, fords the brook and attacks slopes opposite to reach Abney Grange

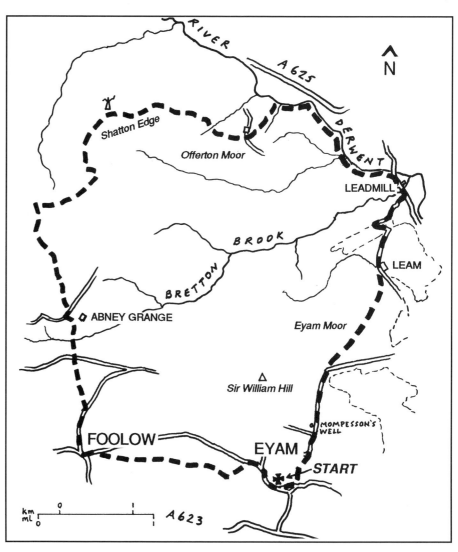

Farm, with or without its endearing free-range pigs I once encountered there! You turn left up a track to the Great Hucklow/Abney road and bear right across it onto a distinct path over Abney Moor. If you hear distant voices or the unaccountable sound of rushing air, watch out for gliders close above you, en route for the Camphill airfield over to the west.

In little more than a mile over grass then bracken, you arrive at a broad track connecting Shatton Moor with the Hope valley. Turning right along it near Robin Hood's Cross, you swing round the head of Over Dale and contour just below Shatton Edge. Unseen on heathery ground above stands the summit tumulus on Burton Bole at 1367ft (417m) above sea level and a little further along Shatton Lane you pass a conspicuous mast.

Down beyond a gate the lane becomes surfaced and you cross the ladder stile at an acute bend where a clear path descends through bracken to follow a wall and join the minor road at Offerton. The great sweep of valley unfolding to left and right throughout this passage of the walk is an inspiring sight, its intricacies of human settlement and patterns of cultivation guarded by lofty gritstone edges. Farther afield lies the Great Ridge from Mam Tor to Lose Hill, the long profile of Kinder Scout and even a glimpse of Bleaklow. Particularly in autumn when bracken and trees lend new colour to the landscape, it is a prospect you will hold fondly in memory.

Passing between Offerton House and Offerton Hall and dropping through pasture, you reach the banks of the River Derwent adjacent to stepping stones. An often muddy riverside path now takes you downstream for the better part of $1\frac{1}{2}$ miles (2km), never far from the railway line and valley roads around Hathersage and adding considerably to the range of scenery enjoyed on this ramble.

At Leadmill Bridge, the Plough Inn will revive you should spirits be flagging! A short distance south along the B6001 you turn right past Hazelford Hall and follow the by-road up to Leam Farm. Here a stile on the right provides access to a wide path, initially up by a wall then veering south-west up over the heather-clad shoulder of Eyam Moor. It is dotted with cairns and other signs of early settlement and if you have time (and compass skills) it is possible to locate the Bronze Age stone circle marked prominently on maps. Views across to Curbar and Froggatt Edges and back beyond Hathersage to the unmistakable rim of Stanage Edge increase in scope and beauty as you gain height: all in all, it is a climb to savour!

From the road junction east of Sir William Hill you continue ahead in the same direction, following the road back towards Eyam village. Halfway down on the left, set back in fields, are the remains of New Engine Mine, the deepest lead workings in Derbyshire at 1092ft (333m); the shaft was sunk in 1860 and remained operational for 24 years.

A short grassy lane on your right 250m further downhill leads to Mompesson's Well, one of the exchange points for supplies and money during Eyam's self-imposed isolation during 1666. Ignoring the Bretton road, you soon reach steeper ground where Hollow Brook cuts into Eyam Edge scarp. Off the road's right-hand bend, a short cut path brings you directly down to a lane at Town End and thence to the centre of Eyam where pub and cafe await your patronage!

With classic views of the eastern gritstone edges, the climb onto Eyam Moor is one to savour.

WALK 18: *Shining Tor and the Goyt Valley*

Start/Finish: Taxal. **Access:** 1 mile (1.5km) south of Whaley Bridge via Horwich End. Nearest railway station—Whaley Bridge. **Distance:** 10½ miles (17km)—allow 4 to 5 hours. **Terrain:** Well defined paths and tracks along a ridge and valley; wet in places. A little quiet road walking. **Maps:** OS Landranger Sheets 118 and 119. Outdoor Leisure White Peak.

It is not surprising that the Goyt valley, situated on the doorstep of Macclesfield and Stockport, should receive large numbers of visitors. Indeed, this has been the case for many years and would have resulted in intolerable traffic congestion had the National Park Board and Countryside Commission not intervened back in 1970.

The Goyt Valley Traffic Experiment restricted vehicular access at peak times, effectively separating walkers and motorists and providing a minibus shuttle service instead. The scheme's unqualified success rescued the valley from the deleterious effects of its own popularity and continues to ensure that when pressure on the environment is greatest (summer Sundays and Bank Holidays), enjoyment is not sacrificed—as it is in so many otherwise beautiful places—to the tyranny of the motor car. A similar traffic management scheme operates

Facing page: **On the descent to Errwood Reservoir in the Goyt valley.**

Below: **Youngsters learning the rudiments of climbing at Windgather Rocks.**

successfully in the Derwent valley, where there are several parallels.

If you prefer some measure of solitude, I would save this walk for a midweek, off-season day, though once you gain the heights there is plenty of space for everyone. Before describing the route in detail, a few notes concerning the Goyt valley itself will set the scene: the appearance and usage of the landscape have undergone radical change over the past half-century.

When valleys are flooded to form reservoirs, not only living communities are lost but with them the tangible signs of man's history. All continuity too is lost and what went before is substantiated merely by written records and fading memories. Farming once thrived here, as did a little industrial enterprise in the incongruous form of paint and gunpowder manufacturing! Errwood Hall, a splendid Victorian mansion set amongst banks of rhododendrons and azaleas, was the home of Samuel Grimshawe; within the complex of buildings put up around 1830 were servants' cottages, a private school, a small coal pit and a watermill.

Everything changed when the Fernilee and Errwood reservoirs were constructed in 1938 and 1967 respectively to provide water for the Stockport area. Having acted as a youth hostel for a time, Errwood Hall was finally

demolished to safeguard water purity; some 15 farmsteads and the pretty hamlet of Goyt's Bridge disappeared, and the valley thus lost its human soul. People are still very much in evidence, but they represent a mobile, leisure-seeking society who come to fish, sail, walk or picnic, returning home at the end of the day.

The walk takes on two distinct aspects—half ridge, half valley. It starts opposite St. James' church at Taxal where there is car parking space, with the added attraction of a nearby pub, The Chimes. South from the church and just beyond the Rectory, a field path strikes uphill to a minor road contouring along the flanks of Taxal Moor. Within a kilometre or so to the left, and not far short of the road's end at Goyt Forest, you turn up right to reach a ladder stile on the ridge-top. Already, across the deep-pile rug of massed conifers, Windgather Rocks' crest beckons, and the fence-side path soon brings you along to this popular gritstone climbing crag. Views from your airy perch are extensive.

A stile at the far end marks the start of a concessionary path beside the Kettleshulme road (but inside the Forestry Commission boundary—much preferable to treading tarmac) and over pastureland to The Street, a Roman Road. Turning up right to the site of Pym's Chair (a stone seat now destroyed)

you will spot a signpost directing you on up the ascending ridge line, with Cats and Shining tors the immediate objective.

Ways of considerable antiquity can often be found on ridges where the going is firmer. Undergrowth too would have been less obstructive and less likely to conceal dangerous animals in days before the great forests which once clothed these moors were depleted. Oldgate Nick stood on an old salt route from Cheshire to Chesterfield, while the Windgather to Shining Tor ridge forms a section of the ancient Macclesfield Forest Ridgeway. The ridge also demarcates the modern county border between Derbyshire and Cheshire.

Rising to Cats Tor (1706ft—520m) and continuing south along a frequently squelchy path, views of the Goyt valley are disappointingly cut off by the intervening high ground of Hoo Moor, as they have been ever since Windgather Rocks. Dropping to a saddle—The Tors—and climbing for another ¾ mile or so brings you to the walk's highest point. A ladder stile allows access to the triangulation pillar on Shining Tor (1834ft—559m), a sombre sprawl of wet moorland dropping more rockily to the Dean valley. Fine views over the rolling corrugations of westernmost Peakland—emphatically segregated from White Peak limestone by the long Axe Edge/Morridge ridge—culminate in the graceful and unmistakable summit of Shutlingsloe.

Back across the stile, you stride off downhill by a wall on a scarred path to its junction with a clear track coming up from the right. Less than a mile south from here stands the Cat and Fiddle Inn, its position betrayed by a prominent mast. Its odd name thought to have derived from a photograph of a cat posed with a violin given to the landlord by the Duke of Devonshire in 1857; the image is immortalised in a wall plaque. At 1690ft (515m) above sea level, it is the second highest public house in England after the Tan Hill Inn in Yorkshire. If you've an hour or so to spare it provides halfway refreshments, being a well patronised hostelry on the high-level A537 Macclesfield to Buxton road. To reach it you simply turn right, descending gradually with a ruined wall then a fence above the Shining Tor Restaurant, to join a cobbled track pre-dating the 1759 turnpike road; the last 250m are along the main road verge.

With a vast, swelling moorland horizon encircling the Goyt's headwaters (a principal source of the Mersey) to the east, the way now sets off towards Errwood Reservoir. For most of the descent you are walking parallel to Shooter's Clough, but lower down you diverge away over steep pasture to the Goyt valley road.

The Errwood Hall Forest Trail from Shooter's Clough Bridge takes in the vaguely melancholy environs of this once stately pile and would make an interesting half-hour's diversion. On a small hill are tombs of the Grimshawe family and some of their staff; nearby are various ruins of cottages and the Hall itself, all emblazoned during June with the riotous colours of many thousands of rhododendron bushes. An adjacent car park and picnic area ensures the visiting public are tidily accommodated.

About 600m north, opposite the Sailing Club buildings, the Errwood Reservoir road swings up left as The Street, previously encountered at Pym's Chair. Branching right, you follow the dam road for a short distance, fork off left then right, down over pasture and through woods to the cinder track alongside Fernilee Reservoir. Reaching Deep Clough you are best climbing up left to join a lane running along the afforested slopes of Hoo Moor at mid-height.

On the reservoir's opposite shore, and not granted public access, lies the dismantled trackbed of the Cromford and Highpeak Railway. East of Buxton it has been adopted as an official trail for walkers, cyclists and horse-riders—one of three such routes in the National Park—and sections are incorporated into other classic walks in this book.

In fact, the railway was completed in 1830 and adheres more to the tenets of canal builders (a then common method of transportation) than to railway technology which was in its infancy. As a result, curves were perilously tight for rolling stock to negotiate once conventional locomotives had replaced the original horse-drawn vehicles. Between the Cromford and Peak Forest canal termini which the line was conceived to connect, a cable system powered by stationary steam engines was employed to haul wagons up inclined planes; rather like canal locks, they raised the track's elevation almost 1000ft (310m) during its cross-country course.

Sweeping south of Buxton through a now blocked tunnel beneath Burbage Edge, and meandering sinuously across the White Peak landscape, the railway proved unreliable as demands upon it increased. After 62 operating years, only 22 carrying passengers, the line finally closed in 1892 though a small section remained in use until 1967.

At the Oldfield Farm lane you turn right, following the access track as it veers round left to Mill Clough Bridge. Rising to an acute bend, the concluding stage of the walk passes through a succession of gates and stiles over pasture and reaches a surfaced lane from Overton Hall Farm. Beyond a small stream,

only a few hundred metres separate you from the starting point at Taxal.

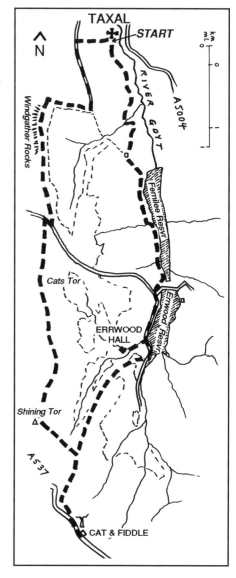

Facing page: **The jumbled summit of Over Owler Tor.**

WALK 19: *Hathersage Moor, Longshaw Park and Padley Gorge*

Start/Finish: Surprise View car park. **Access:** Situated on the A625 between Hathersage and Sheffield. Nearest railway station—Grindleford.
Distance: 5½ miles (9km)—allow 3 to 4 hours. **Terrain:** Rough paths and tracks, exposed over moorland, sheltered lower down. **Maps:** OS Landranger Sheet 119. Outdoor Leisure White Peak (in part).

For such a short outing, this walk embraces a rich diversity of landscapes and features of interest, as well as passing close to no less than three refreshment places! A pocket of moorland above Hathersage, riven by the valley of Burbage Brook, contains many weathered gritstone tors and an interesting hill fort, while further south you enter the intimate wooded recesses of Longshaw Country Park and Padley Gorge.

You could as easily start from the car park adjacent to the Fox House Inn on the A625 near Longshaw Lodge, or from Grindleford Station which boasts a cafe much patronised by hikers and cyclists either waiting for trains or simply 'en route'. But the Surprise View car park east of Millstone Edge offers immediate access to the moortops whose extraordinary rock formations and spacious views will quicken the pulse, leaving the walk's second—and very different—part to be savoured, perhaps, at a more leisurely pace.

By crossing either of the two stiles in the car park fence and heading uphill through birch woods, you will break through a low rim of gritstone onto a heather covered plateau. The minor edge on your left runs roughly parallel to the sheer walls of Millstone Edge itself, a

few hundred metres to the west. Occasional millstone rejects scattered about the area are the rather poignant remains of a once thriving industry whose ultimate decline is attributable to the introduction of roller mills around 1862.

A well defined path now trends left past the massive, layered bulk of Mother Cap and up to the jumbled summit of Over Owler Tor. On the way, look for the 'Smiling Tortoise' on your left, its expresssion unfortunately and unnecessarily reinforced by the scratchings of mindless passers-by. Such criticism can be levelled at all purveyors of graffiti who bring their selfish vandalism into the hills, and yet another example confronts you on Over Owler Tor itself.

Views from the grey-brown boulders are exceptionally wide-ranging, though familiar profiles such as Mam Tor, Win and Lose hills and the moors above Edale require good visibility for positive identification. A mile or more away to the north-east, Burbage Rocks define the upper limit of the Burbage Brook valley, soon to be witnessed at closer quarters.

Keeping to the ridge top through heather, you pass Winyard's Nick then drop towards

a walled enclosure. At its far end, a broad trod coming up from Millstone Edge is joined, swinging right over brackeny slopes to the summit of Higger Tor (1390ft—424m), with its distinctive Leaning Tower rock 45ft (14m) high and overhanging 15ft (4.5m) at its base.

Both Higger Tor and Carl Wark hill fort suffer from chronic over-use by interested visitors. It is, of course, an intractable problem and one which poses a dilemma for the National Park authorities whose joint remit to provide public access and to protect the environment sometimes seems to contain a fundamental contradiction. As always, the advice is to tread carefully and keep to the existing paths as far as possible so that they do not widen laterally.

A graphic example of this is provided by the onward, bouldery path down Higger Tor's south ridge. Marshy ground separates it from Carl Wark, a two-acre defensive hill fortification of somewhat mysterious origins. For many years, the bouldery walls—largely reconstructed—were thought to date back to Iron Age, Celtic times, but recent studies suggest a post-Roman, Dark Ages dating, perhaps fifth or sixth century. It is, in any case, a classic of its kind and oft-inspected by field study groups.

Another scrambly descent is followed by yet more serious path erosion as you cross Burbage Brook and turn right along the green Duke of Rutland's Drive which runs back beneath Burbage Rocks to the valley head. Once over the A625, you are in Longshaw Country Park—1500 acres of woodland and open moor now owned by the National Trust.

Leading you left through pinewoods, the path soon arrives at the B6521 a short distance from the Fox House Inn, first of the possible refreshment stops! Across the road is the entrance to Longshaw Lodge, built in 1827 as a shooting lodge for the Dukes of Rutland. You follow its driveway to the National Trust cafe, shop and information centre (open April to October), branching right below the garden wall to a gate.

Beyond Rhododendron Walk—a symphony of colour and fragrance in June—you will reach a lake by Granby Wood and a possible short-cut back to the Surprise View car park if required. Otherwise the way descends past Sheffield Plantation, stays above precipitous Yarncliff Wood and finally veers down right to reach the B6521 above Grindleford Station.

Bamford Edge (top left) and the distant Derwent moors, from Over Owler Tor.

I recommend carrying on down to the station cafe which, rain or shine, always seems a down-to-earth welcoming sort of place, whatever mode of transport you may have arrived in!

Before leaving the vicinity, many walkers make the short detour to see Padley Chapel. Totley Tunnel, seen along the way from the bridge over the railway, holds a particular fascination: completed in 1894, the tunnel is Britain's second longest at 3 miles 950 yards. From an old mill opposite the station, the track continues westwards to Padley Chapel—all that is left of a manor house built in the fourteenth century by the Padley family, devout Roman Catholics.

On July 12th 1588, two Jesuit priests—Nicholas Garlick and Robert Ludlam—were arrested after hiding here and taken to Derby where, 12 days later, they were hung, drawn and quartered. The manor's owner died in the Tower of London in 1591 and the house was eventually sold 66 years later. In 1933 it was purchased by the Roman Catholic Nottingham Diocese who converted what had become a cowshed and had later housed navvies digging Totley Tunnel into the charming little chapel we see today. A pilgrimage is held each July to commemorate the two priests who were taken from here to be executed.

Steps must now be retraced to the mill, whence, at first, you take to the old carriageway up Padley Gorge. Beyond a fence stile, you fork left down to a footbridge over Burbage Brook, whereafter the initially stepped and zig-zag path mounts Padley Gorge beside waters tumbling through a chaos of gritstone boulders. In places where the ground is too steep and rocky to have been grazed by sheep, relics of ancient natural woodland have survived—mixtures of sessile oak, birch, rowan and alder. Oaks, in particular, support many insect species which, in turn, attract birds such as the tit family, redstarts, warblers, woodpeckers, wrens and flycatchers.

Out above the treeline at Lawrence Field, still in close company with Burbage Brook, you pass near vaguely defined traces of early village settlements—stones and mounds on scrubby hillside. Adjacent to a footbridge, the route strikes left up Hollow Gate, one of innumerable old tracks worn into the surface of the land by centuries of use in ages past. It winds uphill and reaches the A625—its modern day equivalent—at a kissing gate opposite the start at Surprise View.

Padley Chapel.

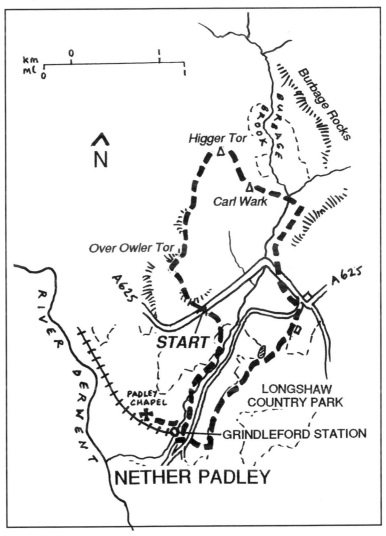

81

WALK 20: *Hathersage and Stanage Edge*

Start/Finish: Hathersage village centre car park. **Access:** On the A625 between Sheffield and Hope. Nearest railway station—Hathersage. **Distance:** 11 miles (18km)—allow 4½ to 5 hours. **Terrain:** Paths and tracks over fields, through bracken and heather and along an open, mainly level gritstone edge. One ascent and equivalent descent. **Maps:** OS Landranger Sheet 110. Pathfinder Sheet SK 28/38.

Stanage Edge is synonymous with gritstone climbing and there are few days in the year when the jangling of the rock athlete's gear cannot be heard somewhere on its 3 miles (5km) of crags. Of all the eastern edges, Stanage must rank as the most impressive from a walker's point of view too, for within sight from the exhilarating high-level track is an enormous span of countryside.

Several 'Access to Open Country' points exist close to the edge, so enabling shorter expeditions than this one to be planned if time is at a premium. However, there is considerable satisfaction to be gained from climbing the 1000ft (330m) or so to the brink of Stanage from the Derwent valley at Hathersage. This claim is made not for masochistic reasons, but because this great rocky bastion deserves to be placed in context as a dominating feature worthy of being approached circumspectly and with the expenditure of some effort—rather like the respect one shows a mountain. Such thoughts do not apply to climbers, of course: their activity is focused at close range on the gritstone wall whereas walking is all about changing perspectives produced by moving through a landscape.

Other than Stanage Edge, the attractions of Hathersage are mainly historical. Elizabethan North Lees Hall and Moorseats, both set on hillside above the village, figure in Charlotte Brontë's novel *Jane Eyre*, written after the novelist had visited Hathersage in 1845. North Lees Hall was purchased by the Peak Park Board in 1971 and is tenanted as a farm, part of which is open to the public. St. Michael's Church is well worth seeing. Apart from a chancel window transferred from Derwent parish church before the reservoir waters closed in, there are monuments and brasses of the Eyre family. Outside in the churchyard lies Little John's Grave—the area abounds in associations with Robin Hood and his Merry Men.

Hathersage is a sizeable, bustling place, less than a dozen miles from Sheffield to which it

Facing page: **One of many discarded millstones beneath High Neb.**

Right above: **Looking west from Stanage Edge. Far distant features include Hope Cement Works (left) and Win Hill Pike (right).**

Right below: **On Jacob's Ladder, a beautifully paved causeway once used to transport millstones.**

is linked by moor road and the century-old railway line from Manchester via the Hope valley. During the nineteenth century, five mills here, whose employees lived in back-to-back dwellings typical of the period, produced pins, needles and wire; four of the mills remain, converted to modern uses.

From the car park just north of the railway station, you cross the main A625 and enter Baulk Lane. Beyond the last two houses, height is gradually gained in the valley of Hood Brook where stiles through pasture lead up past Brookfield Manor to a minor road just where it crosses the brook. You turn right, then left up a surfaced lane by a campsite to North Lees Hall, built by the Eyre family in the late 1500s, though the farm buildings are seventeenth century.

The path continues to climb through pasture, emerging from a wooded dell onto the old Sheffield-Ashopton road (of pre-reservoir importance) by a Mountain Rescue Post (and toilets). Hollin Bank car park lies along to the left but you strike off right before it, gaining Stanage Edge via a plantation and an old, beautifully paved causeway, probably constructed to ease the carriage of millstones and known as Jacob's Ladder.

For a short time you follow the edge-top path left but soon digress downhill with the track running along from Stanedge Pole. Now below the edge, you cross a ladder stile onto a path through heather. On hillside below stands the Buck Stone, a large boulder which acted as a rudimentary shelter for men leading packhorse trains in days preceding road and rail transport.

Discarded millstones litter the pathside beneath High Neb, some lying in the open as if freshly hewn, others piled invisibly in the dense bracken and heather. It was largely the availability of millstone grit for grindstones that established Sheffield as a centre of worldwide renown in the steel and cutlery industries. After the stones had been fashioned to a rough hexagon shape, they were stood on a stone pedestal for circular trimming, flattened on both sides and pierced with a central hole. Far too heavy for packhorses to deal with, finished millstones could be manhandled by rolling and were hauled out by sledge. Foreign imports began to erode demand for local stones by the mid-1700s, causing great resentment among the workers, but in any case the introduction of rolling mills in 1862 sounded the trade's final death knell.

If you care to follow the path onwards, it will trend north and deliver you to the A57 at Moscar, but before that the crags have fizzled out and I recommend you cut up right to gain edge level. This is the walk's turning point and from perusing walls, corners, buttresses and cracks from below—in all probability bedecked with brightly coloured climbing ropes and exponents of that vertical sport—you are transported to a world of unenclosed spaciousness overtopped by no other high ground and flanked on your left by the heathery expanses of Hallam Moor.

With the wind in your hair you now stride south round the shallow jut of Crow Chin, reaching the O.S. column at 1502ft (458m) on High Neb. To the north-west, in good visibility, Win and Lose hills are backed by a corrugation of high moors in the Kinder and Bleaklow massifs, most clearly defined under a mantle of snow.

The rugged, sometimes slabby path continues, eventually converging with and crossing a rising track—the so-called Roman Long Causeway. You could detour along to the left for a look at Stanedge Pole, a strategic landmark for the old packhorse trains from Sheffield, directing them to the correct line over Stanage Edge.

Ahead and below are some of the finest gritstone ramparts in Derbyshire. In all there are over 500 climbing routes of all grades on Stanage. It all began back in 1890 when J.W. Puttrell explored several gulley routes on cliffs virtually untouched by man. Since then a steadily increasing number of climbers, many from the great Sheffield and Manchester conurbations, have turned their attention to this 'local' outcrop, pioneering new and ever harder ascents, particularly since the 1950's and 60's.

Beyond a ledge called Robin Hood's Cave and the second O.S. column, this one fractionally lower at 1500ft (457m), the rocks peter out and are given a full stop, so to speak, in the shape of the Cowper Stone. Our way drops from the O.S. column to a minor road, turns right down past Overstones Farm, swings left at a junction and forks right into a lane. As if underlining the walk's scenic endowment, a splendid prospect suddenly opens up to the west, taking in Lose Hill and the Great Ridge, the Kinder moors and the Hope and Derwent valleys.

Pivoting left all the time, you are taken past Leveret Croft, Kimber Court and Moorseats; from a stile there you enter a metalled, sunken lane ending at St. Michael's churchyard. Continuing down by a wall brings you out to Baulk Lane and the centre of Hathersage.

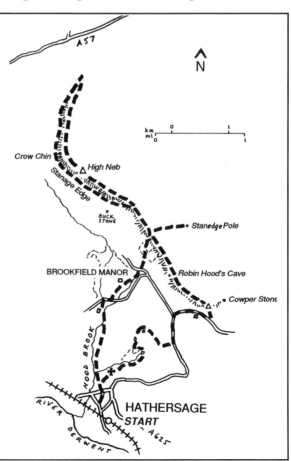

WALK 21: *Castleton, Mam Tor and the Show Caves*

Start/Finish: Castleton car park. **Access:** From the A625 (permanently cut by landslip) in the Hope valley west of Sheffield. Nearest railway stations—Hope and Edale. **Distance:** 6 miles (9.5km)—allow 3 hours plus extra time for sightseeing. **Terrain:** Good paths and tracks with moderate ascents. A steep path off Mam Tor, exposed in rough weather. **Maps:** OS Landranger Sheet 110. Outdoor Leisure Dark Peak.

Uniquely in the Peak District, your attentions on this outing will at times be drawn underground. In addition to fascinating geological surface features where the Park's southern limestone uplands fuse dramatically with the Mam Tor shales, a hidden world of subterranean caverns and old mines awaits. Sir Arthur Conan Doyle said of it: 'All this country is hollow. Could you strike it with a gigantic hammer, it would boom like a drum, or possibly cave in altogether.'

It is not often we may witness the processes of land formation and erosion in such graphic forms as Castleton's show caves, the great crumbling east face of Mam Tor, and Winnats Pass, an extraordinary, canyon-like defile fringed with limestone crags. Within a couple of square miles, history and geology combine to produce one of the most absorbing walks in the whole National Park, and its modest length ensures plenty of time is available for studied reflection on what you see.

Castleton may not have expanded much since its establishment as a planned (rather than randomly extended) township below Peveril Castle in the late 1100s, but today's population is daily swelled by tourists who flock here to experience this hollow landscape at first hand. Yet by the same token it is a welcoming sort of place. There are pubs and cafes,

shops and accommodation—including a youth hostel in seventeenth-century Castleton Hall—and a welcome sense of freedom from through traffic which blighted the village before the earth moved and the A625 hairpin below Mam Tor buckled and cracked beyond repair in 1979.

Use of the 1 in 5 Winnat's Pass is restricted to light vehicles, which is just as well for this ancient thoroughfare—a natural line of weakness in the amphitheatre of steep ground between Lose Hill and Bradwell—has been designated a Site of Special Scientific Interest. With their concentration firmly fixed on negotiating the tricky road, motorists see little of Winnat's scenic qualities: walkers, as usual, have the best of it. Some simple map reading would allow this walk to be shortened to include a walk up (or down) the pass if desired.

Facing page: **Mam Tor summit.**

Below: **'Hollow country' near Treak Cliff Cavern and the Blue John Mine.**

Just over ½ mile along the Winnat's road stands the entrance to Speedwell Mine, where a 104-step descent leads to a subterranean journey by boat. For about 800m you are edged along a canal to the famous Speedwell Cavern, both features at least partially formed by miners working the disastrously unsuccessful Speedwell Lead Mine in the 1770s.

The imposing Norman castle (now in the care of English Heritage) was put up by William the Conqueror's local bailiff, William Peveril, whose special duty was to protect valuable hunting and lead mining rights in the Royal Forest of the Peak. Henry II added the great rectangular keep in 1176, the hall and circular towers being of slightly later date, but by the fourteenth century the stronghold's importance had declined and it was already ruinous by the 1600s. It remains, nonetheless, a supremely evocative ruin, set above the natural moat of Cave Dale and the yawning mouth of Peak Cavern in whose recesses once stood cottages and a rope-makers walkway.

From Castleton's car park you first locate the village centre, walking up Castle Street past the National Park Information Centre and St. Edmund's Parish Church, built by the castle's

masons but subsequently rather heavily restored. Beyond the zig-zag path to Peveril Castle, you proceed left across Market Square towards Bargate to find the incongruously narrow entrance to Cave Dale. Almost immediately, however, there is a widening of the grassy dale which is overtopped by crags of reef limestone formed in an ancient coral sea, and harbours eight caves. As you might expect in such a sheltered sanctuary, evidence of occupation from both the New Stone Age and Bronze Age has been unearthed here.

Eccentric in geological terms, Cave Dale closes in again. Passing through a metal gate, the stony path's slope eases off and further gates lead you out into open pasture to pick up the Dirtlow Rake bridle track on Old Moor—an area littered with disused mine workings and culminating in the vast Eldon Hill quarry complex.

Two hundred metres west you fork right onto Rowter Lane—a mile of easy going to the B6061 with magnificent views forward to Mam Tor and Rushup Edge. Maintaining the same direction to traverse Windy Knoll and the A625 (here resuming its westward course from the hiatus just below), you climb to Mam Nick, the only point where a motor road crosses the Great Ridge.

With sights firmly set upon reaching the summit of Mam Tor at 1695ft (517m), the stepped path will no doubt be attacked with the necessary gusto. However, should very strong winds threaten a safe passage over Mam Tor (it is not uncommon to be unable to stand up on the exposed top!), I recommend you simply divert down the A625 and thus by-pass the hill altogether.

Mam Tor has become a mecca for hang-

Mam Tor's precipitous and unstable east face.

gliders and para-gliding so if conditions are suitable you will encounter in close up what you will already have observed at a distance from Rowter Lane—colourful wings soaring in the updraughts created by the hill's unusual topography.

In good visibility the summit panorama resembles a geography lesson on the Peak District's middle region: from the Kinder and Derwent moors in the north to the Hope valley and gritstone edges in the east, round past the ground just trodden and a hint of the hills above Dove Dale, to Axe Edge, Shining Tor and, nearer at hand, the Great Ridge curving west.

The epithet 'Shivering Mountain' is an apt one, for Mam Tor is composed of horizontal bands of sandstone and soft mudstone. Rain, frost and wind continually nibble away at this unstable layer cake, periodically causing landslips which account for its precipitous east face.

Extreme caution is required when locating the steps off the little summit plateau: the consequences of a fall are unthinkable. Discretion is always the better part of valour, so if in doubt retrace your steps down to the A625. However, in fair conditions the steep southern edge of the cliff is descended, where somewhat easier slopes lead to the A625 near the end of the still motorable section.

It is now necessary to walk up the tarmac (stunning views persist to the north and west) and down the access lane to the Blue John Mine. Blue John (thought to derive from the French 'bleu-jaune' meaning 'blue-yellow') was formed aeons ago when molten minerals from the earth's core were forced up into cracks and fissures within the limestone of Treak Cliff, combining with hydrocarbons and cooling into the beautiful blue, purple, yellow and white banded fluorspar exclusive to this location. From the mid-1700s Blue John was being incorporated into ornaments and used as inlay, with the mines producing up to 20 tons a year. Remaining veins are thin but are still worked for small-scale ornaments and jewellery.

A fee is payable to enter any of the show caves but try to see at least one. The Blue John Mine is not for claustrophobics, especially if you are in a large party. Narrow steps take you down into the very bowels of the earth—an enclosed, dank and cold world, artificially illuminated but quite safe, yet impressively alien if you are unaccustomed to going underground. In addition to Blue John deposits, there are stalagmites and stalagtites and shadowy rock formations to wonder at.

Stiles to the east of the mine lead you round to Treak Cliff Cavern, another subterranean marvel associated with the Blue John industry. Steps below this entrance give out to the ill-fated A625, a turnpike dating from 1817 but rarely free from the threat of landslide. Not far up to the left are the remains of Odin Mine from which prodigious quantities of lead ore were extracted during the late eighteenth and nineteenth centuries. The workings are notoriously hazardous, so any exploration should be tempered with prudence.

To find the footpath route down to Castleton—a more pleasant alternative to the A625—you cross a fence stile, walk through the old spoil enclosure and downhill over bracken to Knowlegates Farm. Now on the right hand side of a shallow valley containing Mam Sitch, the way is defined by a series of field stiles and emerges just west of Castleton village centre.

Facing page: **Lose Hill, seen across the Noe valley from near Hope Cross.**

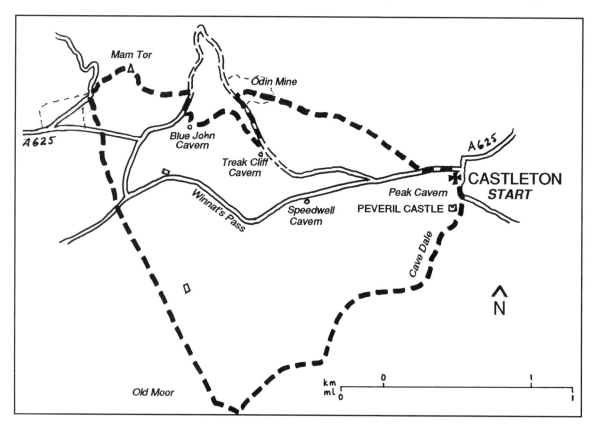

WALK 22: *Lose Hill, Win Hill and the Vale of Edale*

Start/Finish: Hope. **Access:** On the A625 between Sheffield and Chapel-en-le-Frith, 1½ miles (2.5km) east of Castleton. Nearest railway station—Hope. **Distance:** 11 miles (18km)—allow about 5 hours. **Terrain:** Hill and valley-side paths and tracks. Steep ground here and there and an initial ascent of 900ft (274m). **Maps:** OS Landranger Sheet 110. Outdoor Leisure Dark Peak.

Take almost any O.S. map covering a section of this long-settled country of ours and you will discover place names which intrigue. Many derive from Old English and require interpreting, while others pertain to local events, personalities or topographical features.

There are many such names in the Dark Peak—expressive, evocative and curious names such as Lost Lad, Mount Famine, The Swamp, Soldier's Lump, Madwoman's Stones and the ubiquitous Featherbed Moss. In this context I had often wondered about Win and Lose hills, facing each other across the Hope valley at the southern limit of the Dark Peak moors. Who were the victor and vanquished and what race or struggle had they engaged in?

Explanations are rife and ultimately you take your pick from what strikes you as most convincing. According to Mark Richards in his excellent guidebook *High Peak Walks* (Cicerone Press), the earliest recorded references to Win Hill date back seven centuries and appear as 'Wythinehull' meaning 'withy' or 'willow hill'—small pockets of willow still survive in the dense conifer huddle of Winhill Plantation. Others believe 'Win' refers to bilberries.

Lose Hill, Richards proposes, could be a translocated name derived from the Old English 'hlose' meaning 'pig sty', or alternatively 'lluest', Old Welsh for a 'booth' or 'enclosure' in which domestic livestock was corralled against wolves and other predators once roaming the moors.

But the explanation I like best, not necessarily for its scholarly accuracy but because it is the only one that links the two hills, concerns a legend from the Dark Ages. Following the murder of his maidservant Lilla, King Edwin of Northumbria is reputed to have fought a fierce and bloody battle with Cuicholm, King of Wessex, on slopes above the Hope valley. Edwin, whose army had camped on Win Hill, was victorious, while Cuicholm, encamped on Lose Hill, was defeated. Thus coined, the twin hills' names have stuck! It is an appealing story, for one can imagine the opposing forces, ranged on conspicuous summits 2 miles (3km) apart and in full view of each other, weighing up the opposition prior to the military engagement itself!

So much for words and history! A hike over Win and Lose hills could be considerably shorter than this outing, but becoming acquainted with summits is, in my opinion, as much about seeing them from different angles and distances as about simply trudging to the top. With this in mind, the walk loops across to the Vale of Edale's northern flanks, ensuring that low level perspectives are gained as well as exciting views from hilltop to hilltop.

Though dissimilar in terrain, both Win Hill and Lose Hill form the last high ground on ridges, the former thrown down from Kinder Scout between the Woodlands and Noe valleys, the latter bringing to an end the Great Ridge, dealt with elsewhere in this book. Their distinctive profiles make for ready identification from countless viewpoints in the southern Dark Peak and northern White Peak and their modest scale invites ascent. Mind you, each involves about 900ft (274m) of upwards legwork, though the line of march on this itinerary is steep only on the initial climb to Lose Hill and in a few cloughs above the Edale valley.

From the central crossroads in Hope, opposite St. Peter's church, you begin by walking north along the Edale road for approximately 1200m, passing under the cement works railway and branching left at Townhead Bridge. Keeping left at a gate then right, height is gained in earnest, at first up a tree-lined, sunken lane once used by packhorses, then out onto rough pasture. The old track by-passes Lose Hill, but our way lies towards the rounded summit, marked by a stone topograph at 1563ft (476m) above sea level.

The great advantage of attaining isolated viewpoints is being able to enjoy 360-degree panoramas—unlike many loftier locations in the Dark Peak where horizons may be limited by convex shoulders of moorland. Win Hill's rocky little ridge-top, seen almost end on, beckons to the east: in 2 or 3 hours' time you will be approaching it up the long, shallow-angled ridge on the left.

A major, inescapable component in views from Lose Hill are the humpy undulations of the Great Ridge stretching south-west to Lord's Seat and moors enclosing the Vale of Edale. It is in that direction that the walk resumes, down to a stile, between fence and wall, then over Back Tor beside the motheaten edge of Brockett Booth Plantation and down an unprotected rocky slope above sheer, landslipped cliffs.

A gentle up-and-down brings you to Hollins Cross, pedestrian equivalent to Spaghetti Junction! Here, at a natural declivity in the ridge separating Edale from Castleton, paths come and go from every point of the compass. Before Edale's chapel was built in 1633, the nearest consecrated ground was at Hope, so funeral processions faced a crossing of the ridge, using the lower track to avoid Lose Hill summit. There was once a corn mill immediately below Hollins Cross, later a tannery then a cotton mill, all powered in turn by the River Noe. (The building is now converted into holiday accommodation owned by the Landmark Trust). In its heyday at the end of the eight-

St. Peter's Church, Hope.

eenth century, some 100 women were employed at the mill, many walking to work from Castleton in all weathers via Hollins Cross.

Often obtrusive when gazing south, Hope Cement Works sends a plume of white smoke skywards from its tall chimney: it is hard to imagine more uneasy bedfellows than a National Park and this extensive industrial operation. Opened in 1933, 18 years before the Peak District National Park came into existence, it exploits limestone and shale deposits which form the basis for cement. Gradually gnawing its way south, the quarry and its associated works undeniably provide valuable local employment. However, the siting mocks the National Park remit to protect our landscape heritage from development and to provide access for recreational use by the public.

You now depart the Great Ridge and head for the Vale of Edale's green fields. The path angles north-west downhill over rugged ground but eases beyond Hollins Farm barn, becoming a track and crossing the River Noe. If a detour to Edale is envisaged (pubs, cafes, National Park Information Centre) the footpath directly across the valley road will take you there. Otherwise you turn right for about 200m then strike left up the farm lane and over the railway line to Ollerbrook Booth.

At this point commences a traverse of the lower moorsides overlooking both the Edale valley and Lose Hill. A right turn leads you out through fields, past Cotefield, where you veer left, uphill, to an access point gate and a marvellous contouring path round to Rowland Cote youth hostel. Passing in front of the rather imposing building, the way ducks over Lady Booth Brook and swings round a nose of land above Nether Booth. Minor tributary streams interrupt the path at Clough Farm, then you are rising parallel to an intake wall over the shoulder of Nether Moor and down into the depths of Jagger Clough.

Underfoot conditions have grown rough and stony, 'Jagger' referring unequivocally to the track's former use by packhorse trains. Throughout the north of England, ponies were widely used for the transportation of food, raw materials and commodities. In those pre-road and rail days, sturdy animals were imported from Germany where they were known as 'Jaeger' (hunter) ponies, hence the widespread occurrence of Jagger in place names. A footpath running up the clough makes a good line of approach from Hope onto the Kinder plateau, but our itinerary fords the stream to a gate and climbs determinedly to a stile below Crookstone Barn.

This is the other ridge, that belonging to Win Hill and quite different in character from the bare switchback between Lose Hill and Lord's Seat. A short distance to the right you will pass Hope Cross, a restored but nonetheless evocative relic from the medieval packhorse era when it acted as a signpost at the intersection of tracks. Indeed, for a few

hundred metres you are treading a very ancient way, in use since Roman times if not before. However, where it begins to descend towards the Hope valley you stay up alongside the hard edge of conifers which blanket the ridge's eastern slopes down to Ladybower Reservoir.

All along here are splendid views of Lose Hill's clough-riven, grassy cone rising above trees and pastures. You are on the apex of a great southwards curve made by the River Noe, so before it is lost from view, savour the length and breadth of the Edale valley spread out before you.

At Wooler Knoll the way ascends Hope Brink as a delightful green track (curiously not marked on O.S. maps), passes a signpost and cross-path at Thornhill Brink, then makes an obvious beeline for the rocky crest of Win Hill Pike.

It is, of course, the walk's climax. As befits its name, it is an altogether more satisfying summit to have reached than its rounded neighbour, despite being 45ft (14m) lower or thereabouts (different O.S. maps seem unable to agree its exact elevation!) To the west, Lose Hill has rather lost its independence, appear-

ing against a backdrop which embraces Mam Tor and the long skyline of Kinder Scout; north, too, high moors predominate. In the vicinity of the O.S. column there is a little scrambling, while down to the east can be discerned the path from Yorkshire Bridge, in its lower reaches a sweaty toil up through steep Winhill Plantation.

Having taken your fill of this visual feast, you retrace steps to the cross-ridge path and descend on it to the left, confronted by a broad vista of moors above Castleton and Hathersage on the threshold of the White Peak. Further down steep pasture you pass Twitchell Farm, still derelict at my last visit despite intermittent signs that renovation had started. Its access track gives into a lane, curving round beneath the railway line, over Kilhill Bridge and leading you back to the streets of Hope.

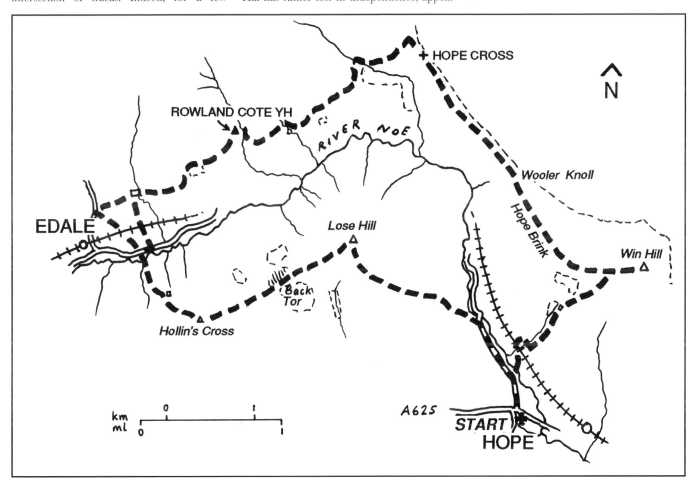

WALK 23: *The Great Ridge*

Start: Car parking 600m west of Barber Booth. **Finish**: Hope village. **Access**: Barber Booth lies near the valley road-end south-west of Edale, also reached from the A625 via Mam Nick. Hope is on the A625, 2 miles east of Castleton. **Distance**: 7 miles (11km)—allow about 4 hours. **Terrain**: A long, undulating ridge with a few sharp ascents. Good paths throughout. **Maps**: OS Landranger Sheet 110. Outdoor Leisure Dark Peak.

Facing page: **After dropping to Mam Nick, the ridge rises to the summit of Mam Tor (top left).**

Between the ancient carboniferous limestone scenery of the White Peak and the sombre gritstone moors in the north runs a high and distinctive ridge. That it separates these two landscape types is appropriate for there is nothing quite like it anywhere else in the Peak District. Its skyline tends to dominate views from the Edale valley which it helps to enclose and invokes a tingle of excitement for travellers approaching from the east who see it dramatically foreshortened.

The Great Ridge, as it is known, extends about 4 miles (6.5km) from Lord's Seat in the west to Lose Hill in the east, taking in the tops of Mam Tor and Back Tor along the way. I have walked it in snow and heavy mist when the sense of exposure, of being suspended between two voids, was far greater than its modest 1000ft (305m) elevation above adjacent valleys would normally create. When Edale and Castleton were once baking under a summer sun, the ridge provided a welcome breeze, while on another occasion an exhilarating tussle with gale force winds (from which there is little shelter) turned the outing into an energy-sapping challenge. It is, indeed, a walk for all seasons.

A traverse of the Great Ridge is often undertaken as part of a circular itinerary since a number of paths climb to its crest from north and south. But although this can be more convenient in some respects, it does dilute the experience of a ridge walk as such. You can readily start the walk at Edale and finish at Hope (or vise versa), returning by train or by road using the 2-car system or the services of a friendly non-walking driver! In fact, it would not become an excessively long hike to traverse the ridge in both directions at one go.

Apart from above crags and outcrops which fringe the great plateaux of Kinder and Bleaklow and which form the eastern gritstone edges, walkers in the Dark Peak encounter relatively few airy situations. The Great Ridge may seem tame by comparison with the Snowdon Horseshoe or Striding Edge in the Lake District, yet it is of immense appeal and interest within the context of walking in the Peak National Park.

There is car parking about 500m west of Barber Booth where the valley road joins that coming down from Mam Nick. Edale's main car park and its railway station are approximately 1 mile (1.5km) distant. Mid-way

between the Mam Nick junction and the arched railway bridge, a path strikes off south-west past Manor House Farm and field enclosures towards the skyline enclosing the Edale valley. As the ground ahead steepens, you join the old Chapel Gate track, an obvious reference to an ancient link with Chapel-en-le-Frith.

Higher up, at a large cairn signposted by the Peak and Northern Footpath Society, you cross the broad saddle of Colborne, beneath which the railway line to Manchester runs in Cowburn Tunnel, and arrive at a track dropping right to the road along Rushup Edge. This track you now follow to the left, alongside an

Above: **The Vale of Edale from Lord's Seat on a hot day in early summer.**

Below: **Descending from Mam Tor towards Hollins Cross. The Derwent moors lie along the far horizon.**

old wall, at the start of the Great Ridge. At first, slopes are too shallow and expansive to feel ridge-like but as you gain height gently there is an appreciable narrowing. From the Bronze Age barrow at 1802ft (549m) on Lord's Seat you have a fine view forward along this rugged spine of land, though none of its more pronounced tops exceed your present elevation.

Of two parallel paths, the higher one is best, taking you above an extensive area of slumped hillocks down to your left—the result of under-mining by meltwater during the last Ice Age. Mam Tor, clearly the next objective, curves impressively ahead but reveals nothing of its eastern precipice. Passing a tree denuded and bent double by the elements, the path drops to a roadside gate at Mam Nick.

From the summit of the road pass, a stile leads to a well made, stepped ascent of Mam Tor. Few paths suffer such an onslaught of human footsteps, for not only is there a large car park in woods just below which encourages the world and his wife to get to the top, but this is also a favoured location for hang-gliding and para-gliding. Since the sport was in its infancy, accessible points along the ridge either side of Mam Nick have attracted participants in considerable numbers during suitable weather conditions. Attire and equipment design grows ever more sophisticated and—the almost inevitable corollary it seems—ever more luridly colourful!

I recall being unable to stand upright in winds on Mam Tor and if it's blowing hard great caution should be exercised when attempting to look down the eastern precipice. Not without good cause is this known as the 'Shivering Mountain'. Rockfalls are common-place as layers of soft shale between the harder sandstone beds crumble away. Occupants of the Late Bronze and Iron Age fort which encloses 16 acres on the summit could never know that by the twentieth century erosion would have taken a huge bite from the hill and would be threatening the rampart ditch itself.

In good visibility, views from the OS pillar on Mam Tor (1695ft—517m,) are magnificent. Beyond the Vale of Edale rises Kinder Scout's southern slopes, while over to the south-east lie Castleton, Peveril Castle and the extra-ordinary declivity of Whinnats. You are half-way along the Great Ridge so there are fascinating perspectives over the walk in both directions.

Continuing forward, the way dips and veers east down to Hollins Cross. The memorial topograph here was installed by the Long Eaton Rambling Club in memory of their founder John Hyett. It is also a point of inter-section for several footpaths linking the Edale valley with Castleton and a splendid viewpoint in its own right. (This is an obvious juncture at which to return to the start should a cur-tailment of the walk be desired).

Rising on the narrower Barker Bank, you soon approach the collapsed north-west flank of Back Tor; the plantation which once lent an air of romance to the imposing cliff now seems rather bedraggled! There ensues a stiff pull up on a badly eroded and stony path, but it is not a long one and thereafter the ridge wall is followed onwards with a fence to your right. Beyond a stile you are freed from this restricting corridor as the wall swings away left and the final, steeper, feet of ascent on the Great Ridge bring you out onto Lose (pronounced 'loose') Hill, at 1563ft (476m) above sea level.

Owned by the National Trust, this is a rounded, grassy summit, quite unlike Win Hill, its sister by association across the River Noe. Equipped with a topograph pillar, Lose Hill is another vantage point 'par excellence', though with the Great Ridge just completed and in view right back to Lord's Seat, that is where your gaze is likely to rest.

All that remains now of this linear traverse is a descent to Hope—a fairly relentless 1000ft (305m). The path leaves south-east past the top of a stream valley—a conspicuous feature seen from the east—crosses a couple of stiles and enters an old sunken lane enclosed by hedges and low trees. At Townhead Bridge you meet the Vale of Edale road where, perhaps, a lift awaits. Travellers by train face a further 1½ miles (2.5km) walk through Hope village, but with the added attraction of obtaining refresh-ments! The somewhat inconveniently situated railway station is off the Hathersage road. Perhaps best known for its Study Centre at Losehill Hall, Hope receives fewer tourists than Edale or nearby Castleton but is no less wel-coming a place and provides a good alterna-tive base from which to explore this part of the Dark Peak.

Facing page: **Intriguing gritstone boulders known as 'Whipsnade' or 'The Woolpacks'.**

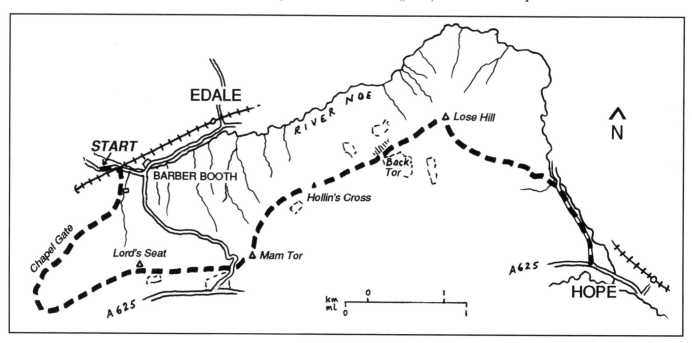

WALK 24: *A Circuit of Edale Head*

Start/Finish: Car park, Barber Booth. **Access:** On the Edale valley road about 1 mile (1.6km) west of Edale. **Distance:** 7½ miles (12km)—allow 4 hours. **Terrain:** One main ascent, then rough, sometimes boggy paths. The latter half along a featureless moorland ridge. **Maps:** OS Landranger Sheet 110. Outdoor Leisure Dark Peak.

can be made without tripping over other walkers' bootlaces! Furthermore, once the plateau is gained, several options exist for extending this walk if conditions and time allow.

Just beyond Barber Booth, the valley road passes beneath the elegant arches of a bridge spanning the Sheffield to Manchester railway line. Three hundred metres further on, a car park has been created on the left and this forms the walk's base. It would be perfectly possible to begin at Edale and take the clear field path round the base of Broadlee Bank to Upper Booth, but this adds a mile of low level walking to each end of the outing.

Initially the minor road is followed to Upper Booth ('booth' being a Tudor word for a temporary herdsmen's shelter, reflecting the pastoral origins of a number of settlements in the Vale of Edale). From a stile beside Crowden Brook road bridge, our path sets off upstream along the west bank to a footbridge then a stile heralding Open Country. Paradoxically, your immediate surroundings close in as height is gained in this secretive and charming clough.

Tributary streams are stepped over and, in one or two places towards the top where the gradient steepens, the main watercourse itself is crossed and recrossed as it gurgles and splashes over rocky steps. Before long the jutting prow of Crowden Tower looms ahead: you can either scramble up the waterfalls to the lip of the ravine—a course requiring some caution in wet or icy conditions—or branch up left under Crowden Tower then contour right to reach the head of Crowden Brook above the steepest ground.

A major extension to the walk for those not averse to 'bog trotting' now follows the main stream out onto the Kinder plateau. On a north-north-west compass bearing over a morass of deep drainage channels ('groughs'), relieved only by stretches of bog, you will (with some relief!) pick up the Kinder River which has carved a reassuringly broad and sandy bed to Kinder Downfall, one of the Peak District's 'tours de force'. (See Walk 26). From here the extension strikes back south to Kinder Low, rejoining the route described below at Swine's Back. The above detour is not recommended in poor visibility or after prolonged rain, neither should you attempt it unless proficient with map and compass and accustomed to rough going!

Some of the most visually entertaining grit-stone outcrops occur just west of Crowden Tower where two arms of Crowden Brook fall over ledges of bedrock. A path leaves to the left, shadowing the plateau edge and leading in a few hundred metres to a landscape of curi-

Above: **Near Upper Booth, morning sunshine warming the frost-gripped moors.**

Below: **The view from Edale Head. Crowden Brook flows down the shadowed valley, centre left.**

Paths at the head of the Edale valley receive rather less attention from walkers than those in the busy Grindsbrook and Great Ridge areas. This may be due to the attributes of Edale village itself luring visitors into walks which set off for high ground in the immediate vicinity of car parking, pubs, cafes and the National Park's Fieldhead Centre.

By comparison, the valley head seems secluded, tucked away as it is a couple of miles to the west at the road end. Of course, the Pennine Way's alternative routing does come through here, but while Grindsbrook is teeming with humanity on fine weekends, an ascent to the Kinder plateau beside Crowden Brook

ously eroded rocks. The Wool Packs (after their resemblance to bundles of fleeces) are also known as Whipsnade, an obvious reference to a miscellany of animal-like forms which the more imaginative among us might discern while scanning the area as they move by.

Next to command attention will be the Pagoda and Pym Chair—both prominent manifestations of weather sculpting and further examples of man's inclination to relate to the natural world by imposing a kind of familiar order on the chaos that surrounds him. None of these extraordinary rock features should be rushed past since they constitute real highlights, not just of this itinerary but of Kinder Scout itself. I have often taken shelter behind one or another of them to enjoy a flask and sand-wiches out of the wind—a strategy I whole-heartedly recommend for it combines expediency with getting to know the rocks' structures and surfaces.

As you drop through an often boggy depres-sion on a wide, eroded path round the upper-most feeder streams of the River Noe, the highest point of land in the entire Peak Dis-trict (2088ft—636m) lies approximately 500m to the north. In truth, unless you are a com-pulsive peak bagger there is little virtue in making the detour: accurate navigation is demanded and even then you may be hard pressed to identify the exact spot in a desert of peat dunes heavily dissected by groughs.

Rising again, you approach Noe Stool, a giant anvil of millstone grit overlooking the infant River Noe at the start of its journey towards Hathersage where it joins the mighty Derwent. Soon, at the central pivot of Edale Head, you will have reached the walk's turn-ing point, both directionally as you begin to swing eastwards, and in the character of the landscape you pass through.

A broken wall accompanies the path to Swine's Back, a distinctive escarpment bear-ing an outcrop called Edale Rocks, whereafter you drop over rough slopes to the old stony packhorse route running across from Edale to Hayfield. With 4 miles (6.5km) remaining, 3 of them (5km) over high moorland, a second major routing alternative now presents itself. If for any reason a descent from the tops and a short-cut return to the start is required, turn left. You will be led down the much-travelled steepness of Jacob's Ladder (I favour the green right-hand path) to Youngate Bridge, an uncommonly well preserved example of a narrow packhorse bridge. Before the advent of rail and road transport, teams of panier-laden pack ponies would have been led across this stream on their journeys from one community to the next, carrying raw materials, food and other commodities. An obvious track continues

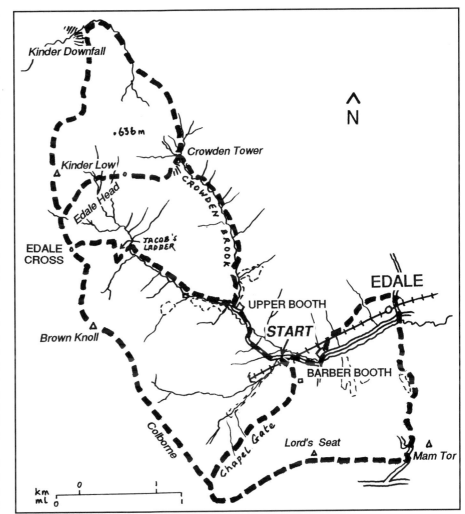

down the valley, passing the National Trust's Lee House and leading to Upper Booth.

The main walk resumes straight up the spongy moor opposite beside a wall. Higher up you trend left (south-south-east) away from the wall on the line of a dike towards the, at first, unseen OS column on Brown Knoll (1866ft—569m) which soon hoves into view.

For the ensuing 2 miles (3.2km), landmarks are few and far between as you traverse the expansive Colborne ridge above the western extremity of the Vale of Edale. It is a natural line for walkers to take yet fails to hold right-of-way status, free passage being granted courtesy of sympathetic landowners. There is a mostly clear path along the ridge these days—this was not always the case—and you would be unlikely to go badly astray even in mist. Nevertheless, there is a noticeably wilder, more remote ambience to this stretch: changes in gradient are subtle, unfolding only gradu-ally as you pick your way across a seeming infinity of soggy emptiness.

The path makes several shallow curves to

retain the highest and least boggy ground, with an overall direction of south-east, while far beneath your feet trains between Manchester and Sheffield run through the 2-mile long (3.2km) Cowburn Tunnel. In the fullness of time you reach a large cairn and signpost where the Chapel Gate track is joined.

A final extension possibility would take you on along Rushup Edge, over Lord's Seat to Mam Nick and thence by descending footpath either to the fleshpots of Edale or west to Barber Booth.

Chapel Gate was the old road from the Edale valley to Chapel-en-le-Frith and on it you now descend the steep northern flanks of Lord's Seat with magnificent views forward across valley fields to the Kinder Scout moorland block. Lower down, a well way-marked path threads over stiles through small field enclosures and passes the buildings of Manor House Farm. It is then but a short dis-tance to the by-road west of Barber Booth where a left turn delivers you under the rail-way to the point of your earlier departure.

WALK 25: *Edale and a Circuit of Grindsbrook Clough*

Start/Finish: Edale car park. **Access:** By minor road from Hope to Chapel-en-le-Frith on the A625. Nearest railway station—Edale. **Distance:** 6 miles (9.5km)—allow 3 to 4 hours. **Terrain:** A steep ascent, then undulations over rocky ground interspersed with peaty sections. **Maps:** OS Landranger Sheet 110. Outdoor Leisure Dark Peak.

Edale, you feel, stands right at the frontier of untamed country. For many who visit the Dark Peak it will be the gateway to an exploration of Kinder Scout on foot. Directly above the village, hillsides rise to rocky outcrops which edge a trackless wasteland of peat hags unseen from below. This inhospitable wilderness is no place for the inexperienced. A desolate and unforgiving environment in all but the most favourable conditions, it will deter the majority of ordinary ramblers, yet good paths around its rim provide access to the heights and spectacular views.

Cattle were bred extensively in the broad Edale valley as far back as the Elizabethan era and settlements suffixed 'booth' on modern maps—Upper Booth, Barber Booth, Ollerbrook Booth, Nether Booth and Grindsbrook Booth (now Edale)—originated as herdsmen's huts or 'bothies'. Today the emphasis has shifted to sheep and, in a modest way, to tourism.

Walkers flock to Edale during the summer months and winter weekends, many using British Rail's line between Manchester and Sheffield. Perhaps because of its lure as a road-end outpost, the village draws in cyclists, motor-cyclists, campers and day trippers too, but weekdays off-season are usually quiet.

Coopers Cafe, a converted railway carriage set back opposite the village school, dispenses hot meals and pints of steaming tea: there is no better ending to cold, wet days on the hill than the welcoming fug created by fellow humans crammed into its cosy, anachronistic interior! The Old Nag's Head, just across the road, and the Rambler Inn (formerly the Church Inn—how fashions change!) nearer the station once shared a common landlord in Fred Heardman, bogtrotter extraordinaire and an ardent campaigner against threatened industrialisation in the valley.

Indeed, the very absence of modern development is one of the Edale valley's most striking features. Roads remain narrow and tortuous and there is none of the razzmatazz you might expect in such a well-visited place—no extension of existing building to house new shops or restaurants, no man-made attractions to clog roads and pollute the valley with noise and litter.

Edale caters for its visitors with Bed and Breakfast accommodation, hotels, outdoor centres, campsites, youth hostel and the Peak Park's Information Centre at Fieldhead. The latter is a model of its kind with a permanent exhibition, maps and books for sale, advice on routes and access, and up-to-date weather forecasts. It is from here that the Peak Park Ranger Service operates—some two dozen full-time staff backed up by about 170 part-timers and 200 Conservation Volunteers.

As well as patrolling the hills and assisting walkers, liaising with local farmers and residents and supervising restoration work on footpaths and the like, Rangers also deal with emergencies such as moorland fires or trapped livestock. Many Rangers also belong to Mountain Rescue teams whose job it is to help those lost, injured or otherwise in danger.

Provided you are properly equipped and the weather is reasonable, this walk should pose no problems. Navigation is straightforward enough as the path encircles a well defined valley, though in thick mist you could go wrong in one or two places. The route's great attractions are its manageable length and ever changing perspectives over the Grindsbrook valley which is in view throughout.

Few outings in the Dark Peak are as universally appealing or as entertaining as this one, climbing as it does almost to the highest part of the Peak District and passing en route gritstone outcrops, rocky ravines and extensive panoramas, given good visibility. With popularity, however, comes erosion from the passage of human feet: sections of path over firm stony going suffer less than those crossing peat and moorland vegetation. Short of introducing draconian restrictions on public access, it is a problem with no easy solution and the best advice is to stay on the main pathways and avoid creating new, parallel trods to the side.

There are spaces for a few cars near the Old Nag's Head and at the Information Centre but they are more often occupied than vacant: better to use the large car park below the railway station and walk up the length of the village.

Beyond the Old Nag's Head, built, it is thought, in 1577 to refresh packhorse drovers transporting Cheshire salt across the Peak, you follow the Pennine Way. Here at the start of its 270-mile (435km) journey to Kirk Yetholm in Scotland, it ducks right at a finger post to cross the famous Log Bridge over the wooded Grindsbrook ravine. A little further on, a waymark post marks our point of divergence off right, uphill over grass to an access stile near a small plantation dedicated to the memory of Fred Heardman.

A footpath used to attack these slopes direct but in recent years a more stable, stepped path has been constructed, zig-zagging up to The Nab. Below you lies the Vale of Edale—pastoral farmland bounded to the south by the Great Ridge from Lord's Seat to Lose Hill: considering your modest altitude it is a truly splendid view.

Above, the path aims northwards over heather, steepening on the eroded spine of Ringing Roger and reaching sentinels of dark gritstone at its summit. Continuing ahead towards the moorland skyline, you will cross a swath of bare sand and weather-blasted stones—a desert in miniature—before arriving

Facing page: **The gritstone outcrop of Nether Tor, Grindslow Knoll in the background.**

Right: **The walk follows the skyline round the Grindsbrook valley, starting point for walkers attempting the Pennine Way.**

at a conspicuous cairn.

From here there is a way east of north to an OS pillar at 1937ft (590m) and on along to Crookstone Knoll, the start of a circumvolution of the entire Kinder plateau, covered elsewhere in this book. This itinerary, however, veers left over peat, crosses the head of Golden Clough and establishes itself on the lip of the Grindsbrook valley by rising to the sombre bastion of Nether Tor.

Nowhere more than on these exposed tops does rock betray its molten origins. Tors, outcrops and boulders may be hard to the touch but their forms are all flowing curves and rounded corners, some reminiscent of pancakes stacked in sagging heaps. Except when heather and ling come into flower, colours are muted and on dull days there seems more than an echo of inner city grime in the dour hues of weather-stained gritstone.

Several stream channels are encountered—squelchy as a rule but nowhere near the impediment to progress of full blown 'groughs', monster drainage channels in the plateau heartland. One or two parallel paths have been trodden in; that nearest the edge gives airy views down to the babbling waters of Grinds Brook, while a line farther back opens up the distant Howden and Derwent moors to the east. If you do not have fellow walkers for company, you will almost certainly have grouse!

Upper Tor is reached and passed—at 1981ft (614m) the highest point on the circuit—and Kinder's far horizon is filled with more gritstone architecture, at a cursory glance for all the world like ruined buildings. Just when the top of Grindsbrook Clough seems but a stone's throw away, you confront a yawning chasm where an arm of the brook cascades south from its moorland source. For 200m you are forced to detour alongside this impressive, rockbound ravine until it becomes possible to pick your way across the slanting beds of rock. Boulders and natural steps help, but if the stream is in spate you will need to cross higher up. Either way, the path resumes, contouring south-west now above Grinds Brook Towers towards the clear objective of Grindslow Knoll.

A basin of peaty ground marks your intersection with the Pennine Way path which, after shadowing Grinds Brook up from Edale, has mounted steep bouldery ground at the valley head and now strikes off over the grough-ridden wilderness towards Kinder Downfall on the western edge. Our walk, however, takes an altogether easier option, swinging left past the curiously shaped Anvil Stone and providing classic views south-east to the Great Ridge and Win Hill.

Past Fox Holes, you are poised excitingly

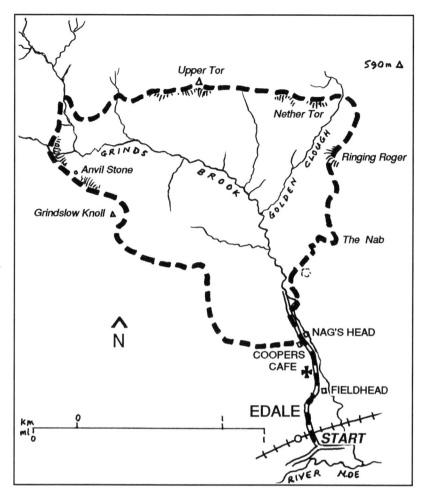

above Grinds Brook whose enclosing slopes fall away quite abruptly. Grindslow Knoll itself is shunned by the narrow flanking path, but a simple detour will take you onto its stony summit. Thereafter, descent begins in earnest. The way down grassy hillsides has become heavily eroded by walkers and in wet weather acts as a watercourse too—a double onslaught.

Lower down, a hollowed track curves round to meet a stile.

Fields continue the return leg, leading you finally into a sunken way between hedged banks from which you emerge, somewhat unexpectedly but very conveniently, near the Old Nag's Head and Coopers Cafe!

Left: **The path above Fox Holes, Lose and Win hills in the distance.**

Facing page: **Seal Edge—a view up Fair Brook in the Woodlands Valley.**

Walk 26: *The Kinder Edges*

Start/Finish: Edale. **Access**: By minor road from Hope or Chapel-en-le-Frith on the A625. Nearest railway station—Edale. **Distance**: 17 miles (28km)—allow a fully day, say 8 or 9 hours. **Terrain**: After the initial ascent, a combination of boggy and rocky paths involving much legwork. Exposed to the elements throughout and not recommended in mist. **Maps**: OS Landranger Sheet 110. Outdoor Leisure Dark Peak.

The Kinder Scout plateau, 5 square miles of heavily dissected peat wilderness, does not invite exploration. True, when you embark upon the Pennine Way you must tackle its 'groughs' and 'hags' (gulleys and banks) as best you may on a compass bearing towards the Kinder River which leads you securely to the plateau edge, but only confirmed bog-trotters will venture there by choice!

To underestimate the difficulties involved in traversing the peat plateaux of Kinder, Bleaklow and Black Hill is to invite disaster. Devoid of landmarks and inhabited only by red grouse and the occasional mountain hare, this kind of terrain is strictly for experienced hillwalkers who are proficient in the use of map and compass. Conditions can be unpredictable and mountain rescue teams are called out with depressing regularity to extricate people who overestimate their own abilities and preparedness.

Following quickly on the heels of such sobering advice, it may come as a surprise to learn that the Kinder plateau does, in fact, offer some of the finest walking in the Dark Peak—not, let me hasten to add, within the soggy central morass but around its perimeter. Here, the exposed gritstone rim provides firmer footing and an entertaining succession of weathered tors—a better defined and altogether more manageable proposition than the equivalent parts of Bleaklow or Black Hill to the north. Eroded peat is still very much in evidence, but a good, if rugged, path has become worn in, giving reassurance in poor visibility.

Some of my most enjoyable days out have been spent on these lofty edges where, especially in fine weather, you can savour a real sense of communion with the natural world. The form, colour and texture of rocks and pathside vegetation are a constant feast for the eyes, while away across vast open spaces lie the profiles of other Dark Peak moors. At such times, with only the buzzing of insects and the occasional passing hiker to interrupt the breeze-filled silence, you would not wish to be anywhere else.

Needless to say, winter imposes a sterner set of constraints upon the walker. Shorter daylight hours and the possibility of severe weather conditions moderate what it is possible to achieve in one day's outing, but winter also brings its own unique attractions. Rough days on the hill reveal the unfamiliar faces of familiar landscapes, no more strikingly than when hard frost or snow clutches the Kinder plateau in an iron grip.

This route is quite a strenuous one by normal walking standards—not because of sustained ascents but from a slow accumulation of small ups and downs as you negotiate stream beds, boggy stretches and minor summits on the often precipitous gritstone escarpment.

Once you have reached the western extremity of Kinder Scout, there are no real short-cut returns to Edale. This was underlined for me a few years ago when my companion twisted his ankle badly west of the Edge above Ashop Clough. We had already misjudged our progress and would have been hard pressed to reach Edale before nightfall, so the injury presented us with a serious dilemma. In fading light, we hobbled down to Ashop Head and descended the Snake Path to the Snake Inn on the A57 where we eventually hitched a circuitous lift back to Edale. Alone or in the rapidly deteriorating weather, my companion may not have had such a straightforward escape.

Edale seems a logical base for this circuit, equipped as it is with car park, railway station, refreshment places and the National Park's Fieldhead Information Centre where an up-to-date weather forecast is available—a vital prerequisite for the walk. The village itself is dealt with more fully in the preamble to Walk 25, as is the initial ascent to Ringing Roger, which is now summarised before the Edges walk is described.

The Old Nag's Head and Coopers Cafe stand at the upper end of Edale and will doubtless sustain you before or after the walk (or both!). Leaving the village at first on the Pennine Way, you cross Grinds Brook but soon fork up right off the main track. A well made path zig-zags up to The Nab then steepens over heather to the rocky spine of Ringing Roger.

A choice of routings now opens up—either

Ladybower Reservoir and Win Hill (centre)—part of an extensive panorama from Crookstone Knoll.

taking you east round the steep, rugged heads of Ollerbrook Clough and Lady Booth Brook and crossing Jaggers Clough to reach Crookstone Knoll; or striking up north-east to the plateau itself and working round the headwater streams of Jaggers Clough on a descending line. Here and there you will pass sizeable pools of brackish water overhung by peat hags, but ways to by-pass them are always present and as a foil for all that softness, there are outcrops of weathered gritstone such as Madwoman's Stones to inspect.

At its eastern end the plateau is almost ridge-like—no more than 500m wide and even less at Crookstone Knoll, compared to more than a mile across further west. There is rough grazing for sheep and a wealth of far-ranging views south towards Ladybower Reservoir, Win Hill, Lose Hill and along the distinctive silhouette of the Great Ridge.

The onward path, having swung west for Blackden Edge, is unclear on the ground for 500m or so but reasserts itself below Madwoman's Stones. Beyond a foreground of coarse grasses, Bleaklow looms on the distant horizon and with firm going underfoot there is time to appreciate your surroundings. Should you consider curtailing the walk, here on Blackden Edge is as good a place as any. If located, an OS pillar at 1937ft (590m) south of the path provides the key to regaining Ringing Roger or the Golden Clough path, either of which will return you swiftly to the Grinds Brook valley.

Perhaps because it forms a lower outlier, I am always inclined to think of Crookstone Knoll as an 'added extra' to the plateau circuit, which is, of course quite wrong as reference to the map will show. However, Blackden Edge does signal the beginning of the finest Edge scenery and the walk could be shortened by cutting across directly from Ringing Roger.

Looping around the head of Blackden Brook, the path reaches Seal Stones high above the Woodlands Valley. Continuing along Seal Edge, eroded peat and innumerable little rocky steps force you to watch your footfalls carefully—progress is certainly not straight-line! That said, you cannot miss the path which stays close above the escarpment past Chinese Wall, over Fair Brook and round the great prow of Fairbrook Naze. Reached by a path from the Snake Inn, this is a popular location for rock climbers.

To your left throughout most of the walk stretches a no-man's land, almost contourless on maps and penetrated only by the snaking tendrils of streams. In theory you could navigate at will from one edge of the plateau to another, choosing which sections of the escarpment to explore. In practice, while this is possible, it is less straightforward than it sounds; walking on a compass bearing becomes surprisingly complicated when you are casting about for detours round impassable groughs or areas of bog. Probably your best chance for a crossing is west-south-west from the top of Fair Brook to pick up the Kinder River bed at Kinder Gates and follow it downstream to Kinder Downfall.

From the Edge (or Black Ashop Edge) at around 2050ft (625m), you may well spot walkers on the popular Snake Path below. In fine holiday weather it can seem like a pedestrian motorway and you will bless your good luck to be striding out over the less frequented heights! It is, however, an interesting thoroughfare in its own right, rising from Hayfield to 1700ft (518m) at Ashop Head before descending to the Snake Inn. ('Snake', as applied to the path and the A57 Manchester road, derives not from a description of their tortuous meanderings but from the Duke of Devonshire's family crest whose design incorporates a snake motif.)

Further gritstone forms decorate the Edge, notably the extraordinary Boxing Gloves Rocks thrusting pugitively skywards, but soon the outcropping subsides. Depending upon the prevailing weather, the ensuing change of direction from west to south-east at Mill Hill Rocks—where the Pennine Way drops and climbs to Mill Hill—can spell relief or increased exposure to the elements. I recall fighting a north-westerly along to this point, only to welcome it as a friend at my back throughout the return leg! As you would expect, 25 years of Pennine Wayfarers' boots have etched a broad scar above Sandy Heys, aggravated by periodic peat fires which destroy the fragile moorland vegetation. During the summer you will undoubtedly have company!

Kinder Downfall is often a focus for ramblers on Kinder Scout, and justly so. It soon appears—a chasm of dark gritstone topped by blocks and flattened boulders into which the peaty waters of Kinder River plunge. If a west or south-westerly gale happens to be blowing, you may witness the waterfall being blasted back in a plume of spray, drenching passers-by above! Equally spectacular are the effects of prolonged freezing when the cascade attracts ice climbers, but in all my visits I have seen neither thanks to our fickle climate!

A clearly defined path heading south to cross Red Brook was adopted as the Alternative Pennine Way routing—a marginally easier line than the direct traverse from Crowden Brook. This you follow to the OS pillar on Kinder Low (actually a shade east of the path). Here the Pennine Way cuts down to Edale Cross and Jacob's Ladder, but you veer east instead past Noe Stool and Pym Chair—gritstone sentinels both—to The Woolpacks. This intriguing menagerie of squatting rocks and boulders is mildly reminiscent of a zoo or grotesque fungi, hence the sobriquets 'Whipsnade' or 'The Mushroom Garden'.

Further on, guarded by Crowden Tower, Crowden Brook bites back far into the plateau. It is crossed above a rocky declivity whereafter, converging with the Pennine Way, you reach the valley of Grinds Brook. It is a fitting finale, water spilling down a rock-girt ravine beneath Grinds Brook Towers and out into the broad, pastoral Vale of Edale to join the River Noe. Ringing Roger, jutting south from the generally east-running plateau edge, is already in sight ahead.

Below left: **Fine walking conditions on the northern escarpment.**

Below right: **Kinder Downfall on a wet, breezy day in January.**

It is necessary to detour some way north in order to negotiate an arm of Grinds Brook, choosing your spot according to conditions, but thereafter a well worn path—several actually—wander along parallel to the widening valley's lip. I suppose you would describe the path as being in a sad state; this is partly due to the intrinsic susceptibility of peat to wear and tear and partly because the circuit of Grinds Brook is in itself such an exhilarating walk.

Around Upper Tor (1981ft—604m), because you have regained the narrowing plateau ridge across from Blackden Edge, there are increasingly wide panoramas north and east to the Howden and Derwent moors. Views south are fringed with weather-sculpted gritstone outcrops, for all the world like stacks of soft, doughy loaves.

Only Nether Tor remains, then you are losing height in earnest beside Golden Clough and watching horizons lift as you drop below 1700ft (518m) for the first time since leaving Ringing Roger earlier in the day. From the base of Golden Chough you are swept back to Edale along the unmistakable Pennine Way path and can duck into pub or cafe with a grin of smug satisfaction on your face!

*Facing page: **A beautiful but essentially man-made landscape—the view north from near Derwent Dam.***

The edge above Grindsbrook signals a final descent to the fleshpots of Edale!

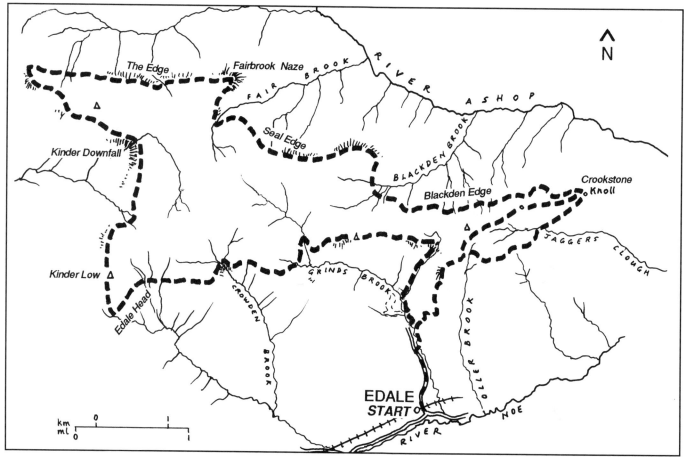

WALK 27: *Derwent Edge, Abbey Brook and the Reservoirs*

Start/Finish: Car park opposite the Ladybower Inn. **Access:** Situated on the A57 Snake Road between Sheffield and Manchester just before the Ladybower Reservoir and the junction with the A6013. Nearest railway station—Bamford. **Distance:** 14 miles (22.5km). **Terrain:** Outward leg—high, exposed and increasingly lonely moorland and a rugged valley descent; return leg—level walking on reservoir roads. **Maps:** OS Landranger Sheet 110. Outdoor Leisure Dark Peak (in part).

Although the outward stage of this exhilarating walk traverses the wild Derwent Moors, its predominant theme is water. Rain, in conjunction with wind and frost, has been instrumental in shaping the weird gritstone outcrops along Derwent Edge. Rainwater, too, not only saturates the mattress of moorland vegetation over which, more often than not, we squelch wetly, but also drains in countless channels downhill to sustain the great Howden, Derwent and Ladybower reservoirs. Indeed, at its farthest point, the walk follows a watercourse down from its remote gathering grounds to the end of its journey in woods 2 miles (3km) away and some 800ft (244m) lower.

It is not a walk—the first part at least—for the unprepared or the inexperienced. As you progress north along Derwent Edge, especially beyond Back Tor, what paths exist are thin and offer little reassurance in bad weather so proficiency with map and compass is essential. In good conditions only the rugged nature of the terrain will moderate your stride, leaving you free to appreciate the solitude and natural grandeur around you. In high winds, rain, mist or snow, go fully equipped—advice that applies to all expeditions over difficult country.

The Ladybower Inn stands beside the A57 Snake Road between Sheffield and Manchester on a small south-eastern arm of Ladybower Reservoir. Behind the building, a path rises westwards below woods over the southernmost thrust of the Derwent Moors and in ½ mile takes you down towards a farm where you swing right, on a track now through woods parallel to the reservoir. At a gate, you emerge into the open as the clear, grassy way leads on above a lower continuation of the woods and climbs beneath the slopes of Lead Hill onto the ridge path at Whinstone Lee Tor.

Ignoring a path to the east—an old route over to Cutthroat Bridge where the A57 crosses Highshaw Clough—you strike out along a curve of high ground flanking the valley of Grains Brook. The Hurkling Stones are first to catch the eye ('hurkling' means bending or crouching over) but are certainly not the most intriguing of the edge's gritstone sculptures. Before long the Wheel Stones appear to the right of the path. Some claim they resemble a coach and horses (their other name) at full gallop, others a stack of wheels.

On a gently rising gradient over heather, the broad path passes White Tor and reaches the celebrated Salt Cellar, a gritstone monolith weathered by centuries of erosion into a multi-layered, almost symmetrical shape reminiscent, indeed, of that familiar condiment receptacle. Down to the west against a background of the Kinder Scout plateau, the waters of Ladybower Reservoir conceal what remains of Derwent

village, submerged when the great dam was constructed between 1935 and 1945. The flooding of the Derwent valley is a story of considerable significance but is best recounted when we reach the reservoirs themselves later in the itinerary.

Dovestone Tor and Cakes of Bread—yet more bouldering challenges and picnic spots out of the wind—follow in quick succession. There can be no mistaking the path, yet already you are diverging away from the Derwent valley towards wide, lonely spaces where

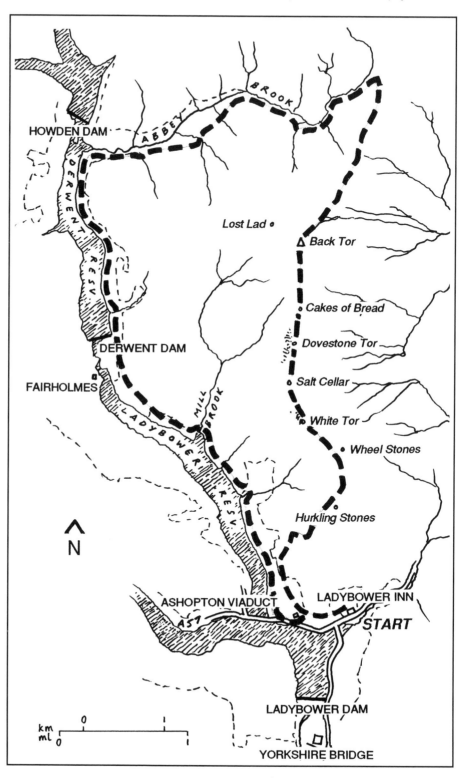

Rock, peat and water beneath a winter sun on Derwent Edge.

human feet tread less often. If a short cut or retreat to shelter lower down is needed, the Bradfield Gate path, crossing the watershed from left to right on the approach to Back Tor, is your best bet, though the initial westward mile round the headwaters of Mill Brook lingers at around 1500ft (457m).

Back Tor, the walk's highest point at 1765ft (538m), represents the northern end of Derwent Edge, though steep, declining hillsides continue a little further. On them, in days when flocks roamed far and wide over these inhospitable tops, a youngster called Abraham became lost in a blizzard while gathering his mother's sheep. He scratched the words 'Lost Lad' on a rock and crawled under it for shelter but was never rescued. Three months later his body was discovered by a passing shepherd. Subsequent generations of shepherds, it is said, have added a stone there, creating the mound which stands next to a modern topograph erected by the Sheffield Clarion Ramblers in memory of W.H. Baxby.

There is a kind of defiant forcefulness about the rock summit of Back Tor which sets it apart, in my view, from other high points in the Dark Peak. A little easy scrambling is required to gain the OS pillar from which views of great range and beauty are obtained. Arriving early one March morning, we found the moors here vibrant with bird life, sheep and mountain hares, the latter still bearing their white winter coats and conspicuously vulnerable against the dark heather.

Ahead lies a boggier prospect and the path is easy to lose in mist; Howshaw and Low tors are minor features in a landscape devoid of reference points. The firmest going will be found on the highest ground but this is not easy to judge unless you have good visibility.

After 1½ miles (2.5km) on a roughly north-north-east bearing, Abbey Brook's upper recesses will be evident over to your left and you can leave the watershed to pick up a thin trod beside the stream. This marks the end of high level walking but the start of a truly delightful hour exploring a major tributary of the Derwent.

You soon enter the deepening ravine of Abbey Brook which grows surprisingly steep-sided. In places it resembles a miniature canyon and the path takes on a distinctly alpine character as it winds along above precipitous drops. At Sheepfold Clough, near the foundations of an old shooting cabin, a geological fault has created a curious ridge at right angles to the main valley and there is an impressive view south to the bastion of Back Tor.

Low trees and bushes begin to colonise either bank as you gradually lose height, passing Berristers Tor and crossing a couple of feeder streams draining acres of tussock grass. Cogman Clough is a slightly grander affair necessitating a small detour upstream, but soon afterwards, on an improving track, you are dropping towards forest at Abbey Bank. At first alongside the boundary wall then through a gateway down into trees, the track delivers you onto the reservoir road just downstream of Howden Dam.

For the next 4 miles (6.5km) you follow the east shores of Derwent and Ladybower reservoirs. As you would expect, walking is easy—always, if imperceptibly, downhill—and provides ample opportunity to contemplate the fate of this once pastoral and inhabited upland valley.

In 1899 the Derwent Valley Water Board was set up to construct reservoirs (originally six but later three) in the Derwent and Ashop valleys to meet increasing demands for water from Sheffield, Derby, Nottingham and Leicester. Howden Reservoir, well up valley beneath the Bleaklow and Howden Moors, was first to be built. Work began in 1901 and the second—Derwent—reservoir followed quickly on its heels. Both were completed by 1916, thanks to a large workforce of navvies and their families who lived in an encampment of nearly 100 corrugated iron huts known as Birchinlee Village or, colloquially, 'Tin City'. The settlement was a complete community, with school, recreation hall, hospital, pub, police station and shops. During the flooding of the upper Derwent valley, only scattered hill farms were submerged, but a far greater sacrifice was called for two decades later.

The seemingly insatiable appetite for water generated by domestic and industrial consumers in the busy midland conurbations led to the third and final reservoir project. Work on Ladybower Dam, downstream of the rural Derwent and Ashopton settlements and some ten farmsteads, started in 1935 and took a decade to complete. Prior to the flooding, houses were demolished but the parish church spire stood proud for a further two years. Derwent Hall, dating from 1672, along with all the familiar features of village life, also disappeared beneath the rising waters, though Derwent's seventeenth-century packhorse bridge was moved for posterity to the valley head at Slippery Stones.

Villagers and farmers thus displaced were rehoused in purpose built accommodation at Yorkshire Bridge, just below Ladybower Dam, but the loss of their homes in such recent times must surely live on in vivid memory. There can be few more nostalgic experiences for local people than to witness the exposure of the village's ruined foundations when the water level falls drastically following periods of exceptionally low rainfall: the last time this occurred was in the summer of 1990.

As you walk south along the firm track beneath Shireowlers Wood, Ouzelden Clough inlet appears across the water, one of numerous indentations in the shoreline caused by the drowning of side valleys. Before long, the rather imposing, castellated superstructure of the Derwent Dam is close at hand. Gritstone for this and Howden Dam—a million and a quarter tons in all—was taken from Grindleford's Bolehill Quarry. My recent visits have coincided with dry weather, but after heavy, prolonged rain or when deep snow is melting, surplus water thunders over the dam's lip in a dramatic wall of foaming water.

Beyond the dam and now beside Ladybower Reservoir, you join a road curving across from Fairholme car park and picnic area—a popular destination for trippers at holiday times. Only Water Authority traffic uses the road so walking is peaceful and you soon reach the outflow of Mill Brook, close to the drowned village of Derwent. Discernible just over ½ mile further on by the water's edge are the remains of walls, gateposts and foundations that were once Grainfoot Farm.

Throughout the reservoir walk, trees feature prominently, either as pockets of shade and shelter enjoyed by passing walkers and cyclists, or as a heavy mantle of conifers rising from distant shorelines. Rhododendrons are well established in many locations and it is essentially a man-made landscape that confronts you—quite different from the mixed woodlands that clothed even the high moors before climatic changes and man's early exploitation of timber led to their eventual disappearance. None of these great artificial lakes support significant populations of water fowl, though teal breed here and a few species overwinter. And while anglers cast their lines, water sports, including bathing, are not allowed.

At Ashopton Viaduct and the A57, the walk is all but finished. A left turn away from the main road leads up past houses to the track along which you set out earlier from the Ladybower Inn.

(The full story of how the Derwent and Woodlands valleys were flooded is told in an excellent booklet—*Silent Valley* by V.J. Hallam, published by Sheaf Publishing and available locally.)

Above left: **The summit of Back Tor, 1765ft (538m)— distinguished by a kind of defiant forcefulness.**

Above right: **Tussock grass in the valley of Abbey Brook.**

Left: **Against a dramatic background of Derwent Edge, the stones of Derwent Hall (centre left) are still discernible when reservoir levels are exceptionally low, as in the autumn of 1990.**

Facing page: **After crossing a high moorland pass, the Snake Path descends to Lady Clough Plantation.**

WALK 28: *The Snake Path*

Start: Hayfield or Bowden Bridge car park. **Finish**: The Snake Pass Inn. **Access**: Hayfield lies on the A624 between Glossop and Chapel-en-le-Frith; nearest railway stations—New Mills and Chinley. The Snake Pass Inn is on the A57 Snake Road between Manchester and Sheffield, east of the Snake Pass; nearest railway station—Edale. **Distance**: 7 miles (11km)—allow about 3 hours. **Terrain**: A clear path across a rough saddle between two stream valleys; boggy in places and one short exposed stretch where the path has eroded. **Maps**: OS Landranger Sheet 110. Outdoor Leisure Dark Peak.

Few classic walks in this collection give you a one-way ticket, for more often than not a return to the starting point can be made over fresh territory. Circular routes eliminate most problems regarding transport and allow for short cuts if time or circumstances become pressing.

However, this itinerary stubbornly insists on being tackled in one direction only. It is far from impossible to devise a return loop, though it would entail climbing to and perhaps traversing the Kinder plateau, treading ground already covered by other walks. The alternative of simply turning round and retracing your steps seems equally unappealing. And so it is that a well-disposed motorist friend will need to be prevailed upon to drive the 12-odd miles (19km) from Hayfield to Glossop and over the Snake Pass to the Snake Pass Inn, there to await your arrival!

Despite the modest elevation reached (1650ft—503m), there is classic form to this walk, one which is frequently encountered in more mountainous country: a minor watershed is crossed at a saddle, or col, between higher ground. The gradient profile could not be simpler.

Should you fail to find space at the Bowden Bridge car park—and it fills up very early most weekends—a slightly longer walk will be necessary from the larger car park in Hayfield—in fact the true start of the Snake Path which has been in use for centuries. Powered by the river Sett whose waters tumble down from the southern edge of Kinder Scout, the town's mills were once busy weaving wool from local sheep that earlier generations had woven on wooden frames in the attic rooms of Hayfield's tall, gritstone houses. After wool came cotton, then calico printing and paper manufacture in the mid-nineteenth century. Only one working paper mill survives, but sheep continue to play a part in the local economy, along with a steady increase in the number of walkers who use the town as a base. Defiant ramblers embarked from Hayfield on the famous Mass Trespass of 24th April 1932, forcing a confrontation with landowners and opening the door to the access movement in this country; a plaque at Bowden Bridge car park commemorates the event.

Downstream from Bowden Bridge, a relic from the days of packhorse trains, stands The Sportsman pub, complementing its counterpart at journey's end and providing a possible refreshment point at the start of this half-day outing. The Snake Path proper, well signed, sets off up Kinder Bank from the minor road east of Hayfield centre. Skirting a hilltop and dropping round to the right, you meet the path ascending from Bowden Bridge. This has

flanked the Kinder Reservoir, passed a water filtration plant and zig-zagged up White Brow above the dam.

Both starts having now united, the way contours along Nab Brow with inspiring views east up the rugged valley carved out by the Kinder River after its convulsive leap from a peat-riven wilderness over the famous Downfall. Height is gained within the unswerving recesses of William Clough towards a narrowing skyline caught between the rounded slopes of Mill Hill and the craggy edges of Sandy Heys and Mill Hill Rocks on Kinder's westernmost arm.

Although trodden by the boots of innumerable walkers—witness the Pennine Way scar which transects at right-angles—a bleakness pervades this upland pass. Indeed, for a time the prosect ahead seems depressingly boggy and it is not until the infant River Ashop has gathered itself from myriad feeder streams and begun to flow with conviction that the Snake Path itself resumes purposefulness. Be thankful you are not pursuing the Pennine Way which squelches up to Mill Hill and over Moss

Castle, only to flounder for a mile through a maze of oozing groughs before gaining the temporary sanctuary of the A57!

Throughout the initial descent, peat-banked side streams are met with regularity: Within Clough, Red Clough, Upper Gate Clough. The going is sinuously entertaining, but beyond a ruined shooting cabin you are led higher above the Ashop and there is a tricky section where the bank has slipped away leaving a poor path which offers little security across the steepness, especially in icy or wet conditions.

With this minor 'mauvais pas' put quickly behind you, a pool then Nether Gate Clough are passed and you are entering Lady Clough Plantation beneath Saukin Ridge. The valley is now considerably more imposing than in its upper reaches and here, at its confluence with the main Woodlands Valley, the Kinder massif imparts a strong presence to the south. A footbridge and a brief climb up through conifers lead you to the busy A57, 300m to the right along which the Snake Pass Inn beckons.

The Snake Pass Inn.

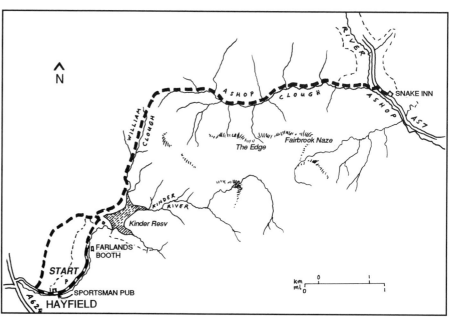

WALK 29: *Alport Castles, Derwent Dale and the Woodlands Valley*

Start/Finish: Alport Bridge. **Access:** On the A57 Sheffield to Manchester road, 2 miles (3km) west of Ladybower Reservoir. Nearest railway station—Edale. **Distance:** 10 miles (16km). **Terrain:** Clear tracks through woods and over low moors plus a little road walking. Three moderate climbs. **Maps:** OS Landranger Sheet 110. Outdoor Leisure Dark Peak.

It is not always easy to find worthwhile outings in the Dark Peak that avoid awkward, boggy ground and that are suitable for most weather conditions. This walk is an exception, however, and as a bonus takes you past one of the country's most spectacular landslips.

Alport Bridge lies on the so-called Snake Road west of Ladybower Reservoir. Both the A57 road and the Snake Inn are named after a snake motif in the Dukes of Devonshire family crest. At the instigation of the 7th Duke of Devonshire, Thomas Telford—that most famous of road builders—constructed the original Turnpike coaching road linking Sheffield with Manchester; it opened in 1821. As highways go, the A57 is a wild and high one, reaching 1680ft (512m) on the central watershed between the Kinder and Bleaklow plateaux. Snow frequently closes it to traffic—by a strange coincidence on the very day I am writing this—but when open it reveals the harsh realities of the exposed moorland environment to passing motorists.

Lower down to the east and frowned upon by the northern buttresses of Kinder Scout, the Woodlands Valley is scattered with farms and dense plantations of conifers. Its river—the Ashop—was dammed to form the Ladybower Reservoir, but in its upper reaches at least it manages to retain some vestiges of self respect as a moorland torrent, despite being shadowed by the main road.

One of two specialised breeds of hardy sheep able to survive the severe winters here originates from the Woodland Valley: it is the distinctive, Roman-nosed Woodlands Whiteface, renowned for its high quality fleece. Incidentally, the other hardy breed is the speckle-faced Derbyshire Gritstone.

Car parking at Alport Bridge is unofficial and rather limited, but the main car park at Birchin Clough, way up beyond the Snake Inn, is too far distant to be of use. Lay-bys beside Ladybower Reservoir could be incorporated into a start from where the route crosses the A57 below Hagg Farm.

From Alport Bridge, at the confluence of the rivers Alport and Ashop, you cross a stone stile and follow a footpath heading uphill to meet the motorable track heading north up Alport Dale, an offshoot of the Woodlands Valley. For a mile or so the going is easy, allowing attention to be given to the increasingly steep slopes of Ashton Tor on your left and to the first tan-talising glimpses of Alport Castles over to the north-east.

Alport Castles Farm at the track's end not only caters for outdoor pursuits, but its barn is the scene of a 'love feast' on the first Sunday of each July. Lest you conjure up images of flower-bedecked hippies congregating in this Peakland backwater for an orgy of sex, drugs and rock 'n' roll, let me hasten to add that in ecclesiastical parlance 'love-feast' translates to 'feast of charity'! This tradition of the rich feeding the poor has clear associations with the Last Supper and formed an important component in the pattern of religious life advocated during the emergence of Methodism in the early 1700s, in particular by the Wesley brothers. Thousands of workers from local farms and industries attended outdoor religious meetings and annual love feasts became firmly established.

It is necessary to double back round behind the buildings to reach the River Alport footbridge, but thereafter a much walked path rises beside a fence over rough ground. Views ahead are monopolised by the shattered rock and slumped hillocks of Alport Castles, but beyond a wall stile you swing round the intervening heights of Little Moor, climb a shallow gully and gain the skyline edge where the landslip's true extent becomes evident.

Here, mellow sandstone walls teeter improbably, overbalancing in geological slow motion. Sliding under the irresistible pull of gravity over an underlying base of shale, whole chunks of hillside have collapsed—notably The Tower, an unstable bastion of crumbling rock surrounded by the debris from centuries of erosion.

With an hour to spare, you could make a brief foray north-west along the undulating ridge above Alport Dale to the OS column at 1661ft (506m) on Westend Moor. It is a lonely place of moorland horizons and gives you a taste of the great Bleaklow massif without the commitment usually required to gain its inner sanctuaries.

At right-angles to the landslip edge at Birchin Hat, a path strikes off north-east beside a ruined wall. It is downhill all the way, growing steeper through Ditch Clough Plantation and brings you onto a track by the River Westend which is followed right, to the road at an arm of Howden Reservoir. About a mile to your left the road ends at King's Tree, a popular setting-off point for hikers on the moors enclosing the higher reaches of the River Derwent.

Our way, however, heads right, below Fox's Piece, to an abrupt turn south where a final glance back over your shoulder will reveal the afforested recesses of upper Howden Reservoir above a foreground of rhododendron bushes. You continue along the little-used road past the imposing grey bulk of Howden Dam which, along with Derwent Dam, began the process of flooding Derwent Dale back in the early years of this century (see Walk 27).

The Tower—an unstable bastion of crumbling sandstone. Alport Castles Farm, scene of an annual 'Love Feast', stands below in the distance.

Threading through mature conifers, the strip of tarmac kinks in round Ouzelden Clough, but within 200m you cut back up right on a signed track towards Lockerbrook. The angle of ascent is quite steep and heavy woodland masks what views there might have been. Eventually, however, you break out onto open slopes above Nabs Wood and dip down to Lockerbrook Youth Adventure Centre.

From a track junction ahead there are interesting views of the Great Ridge looking foreshortened and unfamiliar, and of the Woodlands Valley too. Paths to the left explore a less visited tongue of land caught between two arms of Ladybower Reservoir and not really leading anywhere except to knobbly Crook Hill and grandstand views of Win Hill Pike. To the right, a descent to Rowlee Bridge would give a short-cut back to Alport Bridge if one was needed, but the walk continues forward down a series of tight zig-zags to the A57, passing the access drive to Haggs Farm youth hostel on the way.

In the same general direction across the road, a track dives downhill into undergrowth and trees to the Haggwater footbridge. Loins must be girded up here for a 300ft (92m) wooded ascent to a stile and path intersection at the base of Crookstone Hill. I encountered a group of trail-riders here, possibly within their legal rights but out of touch with the spirit of exploring the countryside in peace. The noise of scrambling machines offends most walkers I know who, like me, go into the hills to escape the inhuman pace and cacophony of modern living and to reaffirm through the deliberate rhythms of walking something of that fundamental relationship between man and the land. I remonstrated with the trail-riders, pointing out how their tyres ripped up the ground and how their motors scared the wits out of wildlife, but I neither expected nor observed any flicker of understanding.

About 250m to the south-east, and worth looking at if you've not been here before, stands Hope Cross, a restored medieval pack-horse signpost set at an old muleteers cross-roads. The ancient rutted track running south-east to Hope and north-west up the Woodlands Valley has been in use for centuries, certainly since Roman times, so you will be treading in the footsteps of countless generations of travellers who passed this way on foot or on horseback.

Retracing steps and pressing ahead up the gentle pastures of Crookstone Hill, you are walking above the Woodlands Valley and having crossed Blackley Clough and begun to lose height below Crookstone Knoll, the valley's configuration is laid out splendidly before you. Coming round the foot of Blackley Hey,

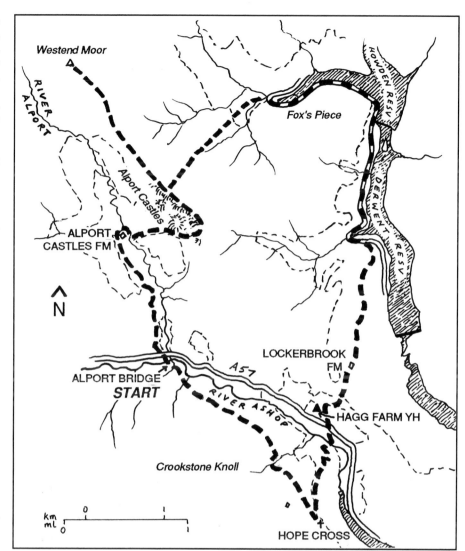

Alport Dale lies ahead and a shallow forked or the footbridge over the River Ashop marks your return to the start at Alport Bridge.

A hardy grazer of high places.

WALK 30: *Bleaklow Head from Old Glossop*

Start/Finish: Old Glossop. **Access**: From the A57 at the western edge of the National Park. Nearest railway station—Glossop. **Distance**: 10 miles (16km)—allow at least 5 hours. **Terrain**: The roughest kind of hill walking over a high, peaty wasteland. No paths in the middle section. **Maps**: OS Landranger Sheet 110. Outdoor Leisure Dark Peak.

Bleaklow (from the Old English for 'dark coloured hill') possesses a formidable reputation among Pennine Wayfarers whose resources are tested by a wilderness of peat groughs and often inclement weather on their first day's hike from Edale to Crowden. Without doubt, Bleaklow can be an intimidating place for those unused to wild country. It would be folly to venture forth without map and compass or appropriate equipment to ensure safe passage; winter expeditions in particular should be taken very seriously.

There are numerous outcrops of weathered gritstone scattered over these high moors, yet one's overriding impression is of a hostile wasteland bereft of distinguishing features and utterly indifferent to the presence of man. Summits, such as there are, do reach over 2000ft (610m) but it is never easy to differentiate levels of ground in this dissected, sprawling desert of peat hags and bog.

I often reflect on how one's perceptions of a walk—the pleasures gained and the memories held—are coloured by the prevailing weather. Lest the foregoing gloomy portrayal of Bleaklow deters you from attempting this classic walk, let me hasten to add that if you choose your day it makes a fascinating and thoroughly memorable hike, full of unexpected insights into this extraordinary upland environment. Good tracks and paths—or, in their absence, reasonably firm going—exist over the greater part of the route, though you may need to do some simple navigating: whatever the season, go prepared for the roughest kind of hill walking!

Several alternative ascents onto the Bleaklow massif present themselves to walkers setting out from Old Glossop. I have not chosen the shortest one but rather that which offers the widest views.

Glossop, situated at the intersection of three turnpike roads, expanded during the textile manufacturing boom of the eighteenth and nineteenth centuries, thanks largely to the ability of Glossop Brook to provide the cotton mills with water power. (You have only to consult the 1:25,000 map to confirm the proliferation of mill buildings around the town). Lord Howard, 11th Duke of Norfolk, laid out an entirely new town, colloquially known as 'Howardstown', to accommodate a burgeoning population, so that the original village— Old Glossop—remained undeveloped. To this day it remains a secluded residential enclave of considerable charm containing a number of seventeenth-century houses clustered around the parish church.

Shepley Street leads hillwards and it is here that cars should be left, taking care not to obstruct access to the Union Carbide factory. You begin by turning left at the factory's east end and following the road round to Charles Street which angles back uphill to a stile. Beyond an old quarry, the sunken walled lane, paved with gritstone slabs, climbs above Edge Plantation and reaches open country; from a fence stile above you steer north-east to Glossop Low Quarries.

Quarry workings here ceased production in the late 1800's but the substantially surfaced lane just ascended bears witness to a once lively industry producing paving flags, stone roofing tiles and stone for building.

Onward progress is complicated by hollows and spoil heaps but not far ahead stands the OS column on Cock Hill (1399ft—426m), whereafter a north-easterly bearing is maintained for about $\frac{1}{2}$ mile over trackless heather

Facing page: **Cotton grass caught in early morning sunshine near Devil's Dyke.**

Right above: **A graphic portrayal of moorland erosion in the upper reaches of Torside Clough.**

Right below: **The Wain Stones, colloquially known as 'The Kiss'.**

and rough grass parallel to a line of grouse-shooting butts. You will pick up a stony track near the broad, tumulus-crowned top of Glossop Low and this, followed to the right, will take you to a ruined shooting cabin.

Still heading north-east, the vestiges of a path appear at last and before long the scenery increases in drama. To the north, Holme Moss television masts punctuate a distant moorland horizon, while nearer at hand Crowden youth hostel can be discerned at the junction of Crowden Brook with the Longdendale valley. But of more immediate interest will be the joining of an unequivocal pathway above Torside Clough just where it sweeps round above a series of narrow buttresses and rock ribs on Clough Edge before plunging down to Torside Reservoir.

Climbing is not done with yet, though for a time the going is level. It would be hard to lose the way, for countless boots have trodden before you (usually in the opposite direction) on this initial leg of the Pennine Way. Torside Castle, a large mound off route to the right, may have been an ancient signal station though any accurate diagnosis appears to have eluded the experts!

The rugged and deeply incised bed of Torside Clough rises to a confluence of tributary streams—principally Wildboar Grain—and having scrambled down into the little ravine you can find a little spring of clear, fresh water, once walled to form a drinking trough for pack ponies and known as John Track Well. Even without horses to tend, grassy levels provide a delightful resting point before the rigours of the Bleaklow plateau are engaged! Across the stream the path continues alongside Wildboar Grain; higher up, the watercourse peters out, giving way to a less determinate landscape of low peaty channels through which the way veers steadily south to arrive at Bleaklow Head (2060ft—628m).

There is no OS pillar to mark the summit with official approval, just a rough cairn atop a peat mound surrounded by stone-dotted, silver-grey sand. The crux of the walk is upon you. Gone are the reassurances of well-worn paths and proximity to civilisation, in their place a couple of miles which typify Bleaklow and which tend to invoke images of desperate struggles for survival enacted in the face of storm and exhaustion!

Although I have always found Bleaklow visually more desolate than Kinder Scout, oddly enough the terrain itself seems more benign, at least in this western sector of the massif: groughs are less deep and there is more firm going in drainage channels. The Bleaklow 'moonscape' demonstrates graphically how the demise of natural woodland—largely

through clearance for animal grazing and man's insatiable appetite for timber, along with climatic changes—has transformed the land from a habitat-rich resource to a barren desert. There remains here an awesome, savage beauty, but it is the dreadful beauty of a skeleton not the joyful bounty of full-blooded life.

A mere 180m away but just out of sight are the Wain Stones, affectionately dubbed 'The Kiss': you will understand why when you head

Facing page: **A typical 'moonscape' on the Bleaklow plateau—awesome beauty devoid of life.**

Below: **At Bleaklow Head cairn; sensible gear includes bog probe, gaiters and rucsac containing other essentials.**

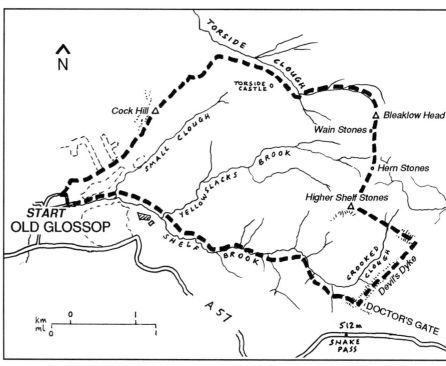

116

off south and see the two weathered rocks in silhouette. In his *Pennine Way Companion*, Alfred Wainwright—that doyen of hillwalkers famed for his immaculately hand-drawn guidebooks—adds to his description of the Wain Stones: 'This is the only bit of sex in the book!'

Given clear visibility the Hern Stones will be in sight ½ mile due south but, although well walked, the intervening ground lacks any reliable trod. The reason quickly becomes clear: everyone makes their own way through the maze of grass-topped peat channels, avoiding murky pools and boot-sucking slime as best they may. Heavy rainfall simply obliterates accumulations of bootprints which might otherwise have formed a path.

Yet another ½ mile of tortuous progress, this time somewhat west of south and away from the line of the Pennine Way, brings you to the OS pillar on Higher Shelf Stones (2038ft—621m). The central Bleaklow plateau, its broad convex shoulders cutting off views of adjacent countryside, changes character as you approach the westernmost slopes, suddenly offering unexpectedly wide vistas. Higher Shelf

Stones must qualify as Bleaklow's finest viewpoint, especially between south and east.

Easy slopes to the south-east are now descended and once over the headwaters of Crooked Clough you follow a prominent dike up onto Alport Low, turning south-west on the Pennine Way path down Devil's Dike. The Dike's origins are lost in the mists of time but it seems likely to have been a boundary trench. Paths thread along both sides and the centre, so finding the easiest ground is a matter for personal judgement. Eventually you reach duckboarding and timber steps, installed to curtail damage on this most erosion-prone of paths, and within 400m you turn right onto a crossing path known as Doctor's Gate.

Opinions differ as to the history of this ancient trade route. For many generations it was considered unequivocally Roman in origin, linking the Navio fort at Hope with Melandra at Glossop, but recent interpretations suggest it may have been a late medieval packhorse road (or 'gate') connecting two remote valleys. Associations with Dr. John Talbot, vicar of Glossop from 1494 to 1550, are enshrined in the track's name. However, whether the parson

regularly used the already surfaced causeway on visits to his father's (the Earl of Shrewsbury) castle in Sheffield, or whether he simply initiated the paving to facilitate trade between Glossopdale and Derwentdale may never be known.

If, over Bleaklow, you have wallowed in peat up to your ankles or worse, then your troubles are at last over! Dry and firm underfoot, Doctor's Gate zig-zags down over Urchin Clough and into the sinuous, grassy valley of Shelf Brook—one of my favourite places in the Dark Peak.

Half a mile or so beyond where the valley floor flattens out adjacent to White Clough, you cross Shelf Brook by footbridge; lower downstream still, the boundary of Open Country is passed and you join a track by a barn. Near Mossy Lea Farm another bridge spans Yellowslacks Brook which cuts a big 'V' into hillsides on your right, then you are almost down at the walk's end, skirting the foot of wooded Shire Hill on a rough road leading quickly back to Shepley Street and Old Glossop.

WALK 31: *The Howden Moors and River Derwent*

Start/Finish: King's Tree, at the road-end alongside Howden Reservoir. **Access**: By minor road north of the A57 at Ladybower Reservoir. NB: Car parking is not allowed during summer Sundays and Bank Holidays when a minibus shuttle operates from Fairholme car park. **Distance**: 14 miles (22.5km)—allow 7 to 8 hours. **Terrain**: Some of the toughest in the entire National Park! A combination of rough paths, usually boggy, stony tracks and exposed moorland ridden with peat hags. Not recommended in poor weather. **Maps**: OS Landranger Sheet 110. Outdoor Leisure Dark Peak.

Facing page: **The moors of Longdendale, seen from Dean Head Stones above the Derwent's headwaters.**

Some of the wildest country in the Peak District occurs between the A57 Snake Road and the A628 from Tintwhistle to Penistone. Alfred Wainwight described the Bleaklow and Howden moors as 'an inhospitable wilderness of peat bogs over which progress on foot is very arduous' and few would argue with him on that score.

If the terrain is unforgiving, it certainly does not lack a savage beauty. Indeed, perhaps its very harshness heightens the senses of those who venture into its secret heartland. It is as well to be versed in the use of map and compass and to pick your day: rain, mist and wind are for hardened bog-trotters in this domain of marsh and cotton grasses, of peat 'groughs' and indeterminate horizons punctuated only by outcrops of weathered gritstone.

Things are not always so bleak, however. During spells of exceptionally dry weather, the peat resembles a firm mattress, simplicity itself to walk on but a real fire hazard. Do not be surprised at such times to find large tracts of moor closed to the public in the hope of preventing another of the catastrophic fires that periodically ravage these uplands.

Dry conditions apart, pedestrian travel is probably easiest under frost and snow, provided the weather itself remains benign. Then, though still potentially strenuous to negotiate, the big peat groughs and the acres of squelchy, boot-sucking bog are frozen into an icy wasteland across which the well prepared may walk with impunity.

North of the Derwent valley dams, the infant river, fed by numerous tributaries, snakes down from its source at Swains Greave, near the heights of Bleaklow. The Derwent watershed (taken in total, a challenging 40-mile 64km hike) swings east then south along the Howden moors and it is this high, lonely wilderness that forms the basis for a truly classic walk.

A great deal depends upon the weather and underfoot conditions. A companion and I were fortunate enough to tackle the route during a winter anticyclone and the following account of our experiences will, I hope, not only clarify the route but will sing the praises of an area often maligned for its grim and forbidding character.

It began with an early morning, white-knuckled drive along the reservoir road, shiny with rutted snow, to the barrier at King's Tree.

A thin haze of ice lay over peat-darkened Howden Reservoir and the hills were gripped in bitter stillness.

Linch Clough is crossed by stone slabs, after which the track runs through conifers to Slippery Stones Bridge. Submerged at its original site in Derwent village by the rising dammed waters, this seventeenth century packhorse bridge was reconstructed here upstream in 1959 to the memory of John Derry. As a former editor of the *Sheffield Independent* and author of *Across the Derbyshire Moors*, his passion for the then forbidden moors fired the imaginations of many a rambler, both from his home town and further afield.

We forked left with the landrover track, away from the rising Cut Gate path, and walked along Swine Side and Oaken Bank in heavy, freezing mist—doubtful whether the day would clear. Swinging west past Stainery Clough, you pass river flats known as Deer Holes, a reference, perhaps, to wild animal populations long since disappeared. Already, in the quiet half-light, we could sense a growing remoteness as we followed the narrowing, babbling Derwent.

Beyond Lower and Upper Small Cloughs— just two of many feeder streams draining moors

Right: **A boundless infinity of snow dunes, criss-crossed by the tracks of birds and animals.**

Below: **Alpine surroundings at Outer Edge; in the distance are the Alport and Bleaklow moors.**

which receive up to 60in (1524mm) of rainfall annually—the track gives out near a small cabin and we picked up a line of old bootprints over a deepening cover of snow. Water seepage from banks and rock steps by the river had frozen into fluted pillars of ice. Soon, the stunted trees which dot the valley sides had given way to anonymous and largely featureless slopes on either side, though above our heads a hint of pearly sunshine revived hopes of blue skies. The going was crisp—a far cry from the usual waterlogged stretches where

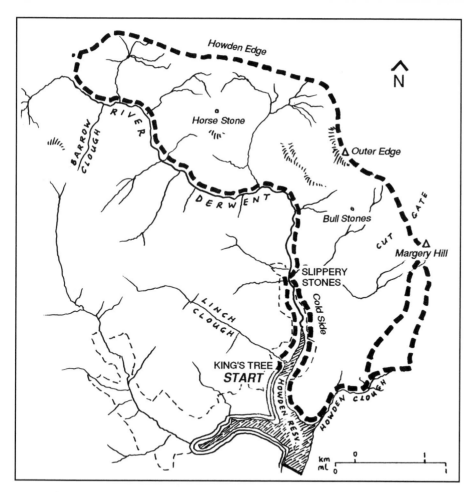

streams join and have to be forded.

Passing Barrow Clough, we pursued the dwindling and by now tortuous Derwent until the little valley tightened and veered south-west into a ravine. With no obvious line ahead on the steep, snow-clad banks, we scaled 30m or so of rough ground to our right, exchanging the relative security of enclosed space for a boundless infinity of snow dunes.

We were close to Dean Head Stones and paused for a flask of coffee while, to our eternal delight, banks of low cloud drifted gently away like a curtain rising for a performance. It was time to strike out north for the watershed proper, shin deep in crystalline snow criss-crossed with the tracks of birds and animals. Back beyond the unseen trench of Longdendale stood Holme Moss television mast and the uncharacteristically white bulk of Black Hill; to the south we could see the Barrow Stones and the uppermost reaches of the River Derwent.

Swinging east on the return leg, a trod of sorts would normally steer you over Featherbed Moss, but that day we enjoyed perfect visibility and could pick our way at will round the hollows and hillocks, keeping broadly to the highest ground over a trackless and dazzling white ocean.

Distant specks in the emptiness ahead grew to a couple walking west, the only other humans we were to encounter that day. Occasional parish boundary stakes (lifesavers in thick mist!) lead on along Howden Edge. We passed north of the Horse Stone and barely noticed the mile and a half to Outer Edge, a sombre gritstone outcrop at 1776ft (541m) above sea level.

Lunch was relished in alpine surroundings, warmed by a feeble sun. Far below lay the Rocking Stones, the Derwent and, away to the west, the Alport and Bleaklow moors; just visible above a level of atmospheric haze rose the Kinder plateau.

The way forward crosses Cut Gate (originally Cart Gate), once a well maintained track for farmers riding over to Penistone Market from the Ashop and Derwent valleys. Still useful to ramblers, it would make a good shortcut onto these unfrequented moors from Slippery Stones Bridge. In summer, cloudberry and cotton grass enliven the shallow slopes of Margery Hill, but we slithered up over sheets of convoluted ice.

There are times when it is pure relief to descend from high ground and a buffeting from the elements, but on that day we were loathe to depart from the windless beauty of it all. Eventually we wallowed down a steep snow slope grown sloppy in the afternoon warmth, and set a bearing along the line of a public footpath shown on the map parallel to the edge and heading for the top of Howden Clough.

Travelling against the grain of the land is invariably hard work and we floundered over unseen stream beds and marshy depressions, cursing the unstable snow crust. Tussock grass further hampered progress above the clough and it would almost certainly have been better to continue along Howden Edge from Margery Hill to Row Top, then to follow the broken wall down to Howden Clough—a routing I would recommend.

Damp and a little weary, we were down past the tiny reservoir and into Clough Wood before the reddening sun had set. Returning to the car via Cold Side and Slippery Stones, the breath of another hard frost was already blowing icily against our faces . . .

WALK 32: *Black Hill and Laddow Rocks*

Start/Finish: Crowden youth hostel car park. **Access:** In the Longdendale valley on the A628 between Penistone and Tintwhistle. Nearest railway station—Glossop. **Distance:** 8½ miles (14.5km)—allow about 5 hours. **Terrain:** Valley and moortop paths, trackless around Black Hill—a mixture of stony ground, marshy moorland and raw peat. **Maps:** OS Landranger Sheet 110. Outdoor Leisure Dark Peak.

There's no doubt that Black Hill enjoys a reputation to match its name! As this walk will reveal, the actual summit is hardly an endearing place: a quagmire of bare, oozing peat surrounds the trig pillar and Pennine Wayfarers consider themselves let off lightly not to have sunk to the knees or worse before making a hasty exit north-west onto Wessenden Head Moor. In the very worst conditions—after heavy rain or melting snow—you can't get near the trig pillar at all and then the headstrong solo walker may run a real risk of becoming trapped in the deep seepage hollows. A more unpleasant scenario is hard to imagine!

As a preamble to a classic walk, this will sound distinctly unpromising, yet there are two good reasons for commending the route. First, Black Hill is the northernmost of a trio of plateaux, each of which in subtly different ways provides walkers with a unique experience of that special brand of wild country for which the Dark Peak is renowned: even Black Hill's summit can be viewed with a certain morbid curiosity as the ultimate peat bog! Second, the walk embraces some truly magnificent scenery, both in the delightful recesses of Crowden Little Brook and over the elevated rim of Laddow Rocks.

In view of the terrain involved, I recommend you choose a fine day for this outing: surroundings are themselves wet and inhospitable enough without the added misery of rain, wind or mist! The Pennine Way and Marsden to Edale trails (along with their alternatives) have done much to tame the Black Hill massif, and paths on a map radiate from the central summit like spokes in a wheel. However, be warned: the sprawling top, devoid of any vegetation across which a trod might become established, is no place to find yourself without map and compass and the ability to use them, especially in poor visibility.

The springboard for this walk is a newish car park adjacent to the youth hostel at Crowden in Longdendale. Signs of the valley's former vigour are hard to find, yet once its farming community, on a trade route into Yorkshire, supported several pubs and boasted a splendid Hall. Manchester's thirst for water transformed all that when, between 1848 and 1877, the engineer John Bateman constructed a series of five reservoirs, drowning farmland and several mills in the process. At the time this chain of dammed lakes over 5 miles (8km) long in total was the most extensive in the world, and even today appears of formidable size. Stretches of water, artificial or otherwise, blend into the landscape happily enough, but I recall seeing Torside Reservoir drained for engineering work a few years ago and being appalled at the massive environmental eyesore

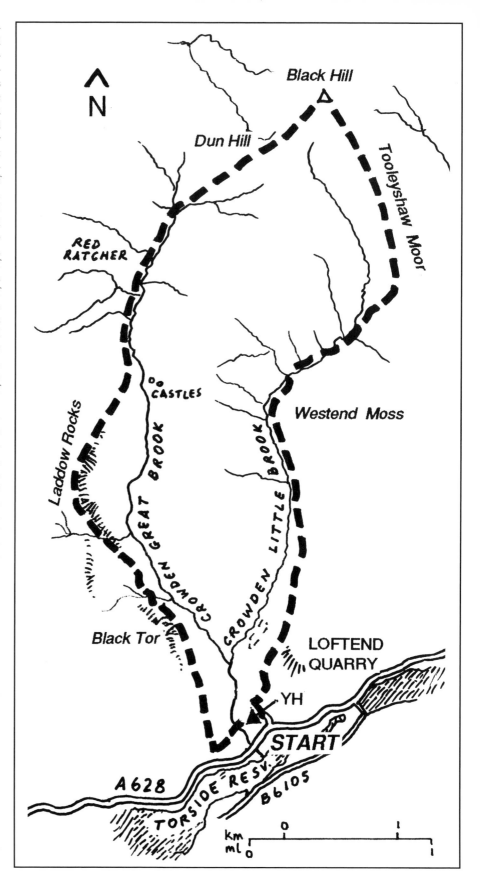

it had become.

Setting off west along the walled lane, you are treading the erstwhile main road from pre-A628 days. Forking right, and right again before the bridge, brings you past an Outdoor Centre and up a steep, eroding path towards Open Country. Beyond the vast spoil heaps of brown-grey blocks at Loftend Quarry you stay on the lower path. Originally made to take shooting parties up the valley to a cabin (long since disappeared), its gently rising course could not be bettered as an introduction to the day's exertions.

Crowden Little Brook gurgles merrily on its way to the taps of Manchester, its feeder streams conveniently running in from the west and therefore not interrupting progress on this enchanting path. Ahead, the valley narrows and as you approach closer to the watercourse, its small-scale intricacies—including a little waterfall—vie for your attention with the now visible Holme Moss television mast on the skyline.

Curving right below the flanks of Westend Moss, the path reaches a sheepfold and promptly gives up the ghost, having fulfilled its mission to connect with the shooting cabin that was sited here. Your aim now is to link up with the well used path on Tooleyshaw Moor some 400ft (122m) up to the right, but there is no immediate rush to desert the infant Crowden Little Brook. Its meanderings are useful for a further 800m or thereabouts, by which point you will have crossed Whitelow Slack—the sole streamlet draining down from the east—and can pick your way up onto the well defined shoulder of Tooleyshaw Moor and the reassurance of a broad, ridgetop path.

Enthusiasm may initially be dampened by the presence of peat hags through which the way seeks out the firmest ground, but there is temporary respite where a previous catastrophic fire has laid bare the underlying rock. Hereabouts the path is marked by cairns but all too soon peat encompasses you as Black Hill summit nears.

At 1908ft (582m), Black Hill was Cheshire's highest top before county boundaries were revised. Its subtitle 'Soldiers Lump' refers to visits by the Corps of Royal Engineers during the original triangulation survey which started in 1784. In 1841, framework timbers for the 36″ Great Ramsden theodolite were found here, the instrument itself now being on display at the Science Museum, Kensington, London.

In earlier centuries, an island of turf saved Black Hill from total infamy and would have offered a crumb of comfort to the military survey personnel. However, over the years what firm ground there once was has suc-cumbed to erosion, greatly exacerbated during the past few decades by countless thousands of summit-bound boots. The trig column now stands forlornly on its exposed concrete foundation, besieged by black slime!

If you are blessed with gentle weather, and if the peat is not so saturated that any thought of exploration is ruled out, it can be educational—even entertaining—to ponder this embodiment of all peat bog nightmares! To quote from Alfred Wainwright's *Pennine Way Companion*: 'Nothing can grow in this acid waste. There is no root-hold in this sea of ooze. In the flutings and ripplings of the surface of the dunes, caused by the action of rain and wind, a certain strange beauty, a patterned sculpturing beyond the skill of man, must, however, be conceded.'

Before long thoughts will turn to a retreat from this hostile place. In the absence of any obvious path, it is necessary to walk on a compass bearing of 233° in order to steer between Meadowgrain Clough and other streams flowing north—a watershed that actually occurs on Dun Hill, $\frac{1}{2}$ mile to the south-west. A tall cairn there, at the head of Far Grain, confirms your position and provides a marvellous picnic spot and viewpoint should the time and conditions be right.

Pennine Wayfarers have worn an unsightly scar in the soggy moorside from Dun Hill to the rising of Crowden Great Brook, key to the descent route. So often on these poorly drained gritstone moors, walking is reduced to a battle against the 'boot in', but as we weave left and right to avoid the wettest patches of ground we destroy a little more of the carpet of vegetation and leave behind us a slightly boggier legacy for those following. Thus, with heavy use, paths grow even wider, posing a problem of increasing magnitude for authorities involved in reconciling public access to these upland environments with the long term preservation of their wild beauty.

Having forded tributary streams below Red Ratcher, you will find the going improving by the minute. Opposite the Castles, a right fork must be watched for: this will take you along the crest of Laddow Rocks on a line infinitely preferable to the over-used lower level path, though in high winds you could resort to the latter.

First explored at the turn of the twentieth century, Laddow Rocks have gained a high reputation among the rock climbing fraternity. There is a cave beneath an overhang at the northern end (whence an undulating climbers' traverse affords excellent close-up views of the gritstone architecture), but because the outcrop is set hard against peaty moorland, the crags are not seen well from the top edge, only from either end. However, expansive horizons more than compensate for this—a broad sweep taking in Black Hill to the north and Bleaklow's impressive bulk to the south.

Once beyond the steep drop to Oaken-clough Brook with its pretty little waterfalls, the way is truly unmissable—a pedestrian highway for those intent on the Pennine Way, Laddow Rocks or itineraries such as this. You come down under Black Tor and out over rough pasture to the old road, turning left to cross Crowden Brook and returning without complication to the start.

Four Railway Trails

With refreshing foresight and official resolve, three disused railway trackbeds which cross the White Peak have been acquired by the National Park authorities and adopted as trails for walkers, cyclists and horse-riders—the fourth having been created by Staffordshire County Council back in 1935.

In truth, few (disused railway enthusiasts excepted) would consider walking long sections when there is so much grand country on either side. However, the tracks offer several unique and important advantages (not applicable to the Monsal Trail): freedom from gradients, easy access and a mostly dry, even surface. Providing straightforward going for the less

Right: **Tissington's Jacobean manor house, seen from the Norman church. This is one of Peakland's most beautiful villages.**

mobile and for inexperienced walkers, the trails run through the heart of the White Peak's finest countryside and embanked stretches often enjoy the best views for miles; and navigation is without difficulty, except perhaps in dense mist when you would need to check your progress carefully against trackside features as they occur.

Cyclists tend to use these trails in greater numbers than walkers (again parts of the Monsal Trail excepted) and machines can be hired at various strategic points. Nevertheless, the cinder trackbeds are energy-absorbing and reduce most cyclists to a sedate pace entirely compatible with fellow walkers: little danger here of being run down by speed merchants!

Probably the most prevalent utilisation of the railway trails by walkers is the integration of stretches of trackbed into cross-country or circular routes, though I know of some who relish the fast, uncomplicated progress these trails for the most part provide. They are not universally liked, but then neither are bog-trotting or rock-climbing: everyone to his own!

The Tissington Trail

Start: Ashbourne.
Finish: Parsley Hay.
Access: Ashbourne lies just outside the southern National Park boundary; nearest railway stations—the Matlock line. Parsley Hay is just off the A515 midway between Ashbourne and Buxton; nearest railway station—Buxton.
Distance: 12 miles (19km)—from 3 to 6 hours depending entirely on pace and stops etc.
Maps: OS Landranger Sheet 119. Outdoor Leisure White Peak.

Running on a course just west of north, the Tissington Trail shadows the River Dove: at one point it is less than ½ mile above Dove Dale, at others it loops 2 or 3 miles (3 to 5km) away across the plateau. This was once the Ashbourne to Buxton line and gains height—imperceptibly to the walker—to join the High Peak Trail south of Parsley Hay.

Ashbourne sits at the frontier between lowland southern Britain and true hill country stretching north as the Pennine chain. Midland red-brick is still in evidence, but the town is distinguished by its market, the splendid

church of St. Oswald, and many Georgian buildings from its eighteenth century heyday as a fashionable social centre. One of Ashbourne's best known traditions, is the annual free-for-all football game between the 'Up'ards' and the 'Down'ards' along the streets and Henmore Brook each Shrove Tuesday and Ash Wednesday—a ritual combat dating back possibly to Roman times.

The trail starts at the Mappleton car park and picnic area by the blocked tunnel west of Dovehouse Green (cycles for hire). Immediately you are out across farmland on the approaches to Dove Dale, but the track curves east around high ground, passing close to the beautiful village of Tissington. With a Norman church, Jacobean manor house, duckpond, village greens and five wells that are 'dressed' in the traditional manner on Ascension Day, exploration is well worth an hour of anyone's time. There is a car park, a picnic site, and refreshments at the old railway station.

Flanking the valley of Bletch Brook, the trail meets then passes beneath the A515 (access car parks) then heads north over open country past tree-crowned hills and widespread views to Biggin and Heathcote. Beyond the car park

And picnic area at Hartington's old station, the final 2 miles (3km) give exhilarating walking, joining the High Peak Trail for arrival at Parsley Hay (cycles for hire).

The High Peak Trail

Start: High Peak Junction.
Finish: Dowlow Farm.
Access: High Peak Junction is adjacent to British Rail's existing branch line to Matlock, and to the A6 south of Matlock; nearest railway stations—Cromford and Whatstandwell. Dowlow Farm is 4½ miles (7km) south-east of Buxton on the A515 near the National Park boundary; nearest railway station—Buxton.
Distance: 17 miles (27.5km)—from 5 to 8 hours depending entirely on pace, stops. etc.
Maps: OS Landranger Sheet 119. Outdoor Leisure White Peak.

Of all the railway trails the High Peak is probably the most fascinating, imbued as it is with a wealth of industrial archaeology. As explained in more detail elsewhere in this book, when it was built the line had been conceived as a waterway to link the Cromford and Peak Forest canals: in the early 1800s, railway technology was still in its infancy and canals were the normal mode of transport for heavy goods. The resulting Cromford and High Peak Railway—one of Britain's earliest—winds through the landscape in steep bends with numerous high embankments, substantial cuttings and stations originally called 'wharves'. Furthermore, much evidence from its working days remain visible at the trackside; Cromford especially contains much of interest from the period, including Richard Arkwright's Cromford Mill, one of the first to use water power.

The Information Centre and Workshops at High Peak Junction (car park/picnic site) are well worth visiting before you set off under the A6 and up Sheep Pastures Incline. Passing more amenities at Black Rock, you continue to Middleton Top's Visitor Centre (cycle hire) and out across the White Peak countryside, entering the National Park N.E. of Parwich.

Impressive embankments precede arrival at the Minninglow picnic site and, shortly after, the Gotham curve, one of the tightest bends ever built into a British railway track and in its time only negotiable by short wheelbase rolling stock. Copses, small hills and superb vistas over the White Peak landscape characterise this middle section of the High Peak Trail: the line was operational until 1967. A couple of miles beyond the Friden works you emerge from a cutting under the A515 to find the Tissington Trail converging from the left; Parsley Hay's car park and picnic area (cycle hire too) is quickly reached.

Owing to extensive limestone quarrying south-east of Buxton (even the National Park boundary skirts this industrial enclave), the High Peak Trail as such ends after a further 3 miles (5km), though the trackbed carries on westwards round Buxton, passes through a tunnel beneath Burbage Edge and runs down the Goyt Valley to Whaley Bridge and the Peak Forest Canal, its original destination.

The Monsal Trail

Start: East of Bakewell.
Finish: Wye Dale.
Access: Bakewell is on the River Wye west of Chesterfield, at the junction of the A6, A619 and B5055; nearest railway stations—Matlock and Grindleford. Wye Dale is 3 miles (5km) east of Buxton on the A6; nearest railway station—Buxton.
Distance: 10 miles (16km)—allow between 4 and 6 hours.
Terrain: Not continuous trackbed owing to unsafe tunnels. The Chee Dale riverside path is rocky, tortuous and involves stepping stones which may be covered when the Wye is full.
Maps: OS Landranger Sheet 119. Outdoor Leisure White Peak.

The best bits of this trail are incorporated into Walks 6 and 10 but its convenient length and enormously varied scenery qualify it as a splendid outing in its own right.

Completed in the 1860s, the London-Midland line from St. Pancras to Manchester ran through a linking succession of delightful rocky dales—Water-cum-Jolly, Litton Dale, Miller's Dale, Chee Dale, Wye Dale and Ashford Dale—on its way between Bakewell and Buxton. It was an engineering nightmare involving the blasting of many tunnels through hillsides above the Wye and the construction of the great Monsal Head viaduct. Of critics there were many, among them John Ruskin, yet what remains today is jealously preserved as part of our industrial heritage.

In 1981 the Peak Park Board reached agreement with British Rail to open the disused trackbed for public leisure use, and the Monsal Trail came into being. It begins just east of Bakewell, the Peak's largest town and headquarters of the Peak Park Joint Planning Board. By visiting the Tourist Information Centre housed in the old Market Hall, much will be gleaned about Bakewell itself and the surrounding area. Many will wish to explore the town before setting out, perhaps sampling one of the famous Bakewell Puddings; Haddon Hall is only a mile to the south.

At first there are few clues to the dramatic scenery in store as the trail curves gently westwards, crossing under or over several roads in the busy corridor near the confluence of the rivers Derwent and Wye. But at Monsal Head (car park, eating places, cycle hire) you cross a blocked tunnel and rejoin the trackbed over the sensational viaduct spanning Monsal Dale.

A footbridge at Cressbrook Mill diverts you from a precarious clifftop path above a long tunnel; instead the walk takes to a concessionary riverside track, resuming the railway trackbed at Litton Mill. All is plain sailing to Miller's Dale where the old Buxton junction station provides car parking (cafe nearby). However, shortly after, yet another impassable tunnel imposes a riverside detour—this one being the walk's highlight.

Although rugged and appreciably more strenuous than trackbed tramping, the way enters Chee Dale gorge, a wooded ravine well known for the rock-climbers' crag of Chee Tor. Some 40 stepping stones along the water's edge lead you past sheer cliffs to rejoin the Monsal Trail for its final 1½ miles (2.5km). The going is rather rough over original railway ballast, but the scenery is unimpeachable.

The Manifold Track

Start: Waterhouses.
Finish: Hulme End.

Access: Waterhouses lies between Leek and Ashbourne on the A523; nearest railway station—Uttoxeter. Hulme End is on the B5054 2 miles (3km) west of Hartington; nearest railway station—Matlock.
Distance: 8 miles (13km)—3 to 5 hours depending on pace, stops, etc.
Maps: OS Landranger Sheet 119. Outdoor Leisure White Peak.

The Leek and Manifold Light Railway was a privately operated, narrow-gauge enterprise that opened in 1904—primarily as a milk train but also to transport ore from Ecton's copper mines and serve the travelling needs of local people. None of these functions proved profitable and the line closed in 1934. With admirable foresight, Staffordshire County Council adopted the trackbed as a public bridleway in 1935 and tarmaced the surface.

In contrast to neighbouring Dove Dale, the Manifold valley winds in broad, expansive curves, joining the River Hamps east of Grindon. In places there is even space enough for a minor road as well as the railway trackbed. The walk is a gentle one, often overtopped by richly wooded hillside with notable limestone crags and caves. Except when the water table is high, the Manifold itself is inclined to flow underground through a system of faults and passages, leaving the bed disappointingly dry.

From the Old Station car park (cycle hire) just east of Waterhouses off the A523, the Manifold Track swings north beside the River Hamps, crossing and re-crossing the riverbed numerous times on its course toward the confluence with the River Manifold at Beeston Tor, a beetling limestone cliff beloved of rock-climbers. Now following the Manifold, you pass Weag's Bridge and thread onwards up the valley whose steep sides deter would-be forays to explore villages such as Grindon and Wetton less than a mile away up on the plateau.

Thor's Cave appears high on the right: it is much visited and is the one obligatory detour for active walkers on this itinerary. Once up there you can climb inside and from its great vaulted entrance gaze over the surrounding countryside. Back on the trail, you will reach Wetton Mill within 20 minutes—a popular refreshment stop during the summer months. Directly above the cafe stands a limestone knoll peppered with caves.

Rounding the northern ridge of Ecton Hill, the track leads out to gentler, rolling countryside characterising the upper reaches of the Dove and Manifold rivers, and concludes at Hulme end car park.

Facing page: **Stanage Edge.**

Long Distance Walks

When perusing a 1″ Tourist map of the Peak District, any number of longer distance walks suggest themselves, borne out by a proliferation of challenge walks over recent years. Because walking in the White Peak is so well catered for in terms of access, waymarking and accommodation, you could wander happily for days, weaving a course through all the best country. Possibilities are no less numerous in the Dark Peak, although there you will need to be prepared for serious hillwalking with a much greater emphasis on self-sufficiency.

There is a certain bravura involved in tackling any of the following routes at one go— particularly Marsden to Edale and the

Derwent Watershed. (see the chapter on Walking Gear and Safety on the Hills). However, if you prefer a more leisurely pace, why not backpack or overnight at youth hostels or bed and breakfast?

The Derwent Watershed

Start/Finish: Yorkshire Bridge.
Access: 1 mile south of the A57 Snake Road at Ladybower Reservoir. Nearest railway station—Hope.
Distance: 40 miles (64km)—between 14 and 20 hours of walking.
Terrain: A long, rough walk, much of it over boggy and peat-lagged ground.
Maps: OS Landranger Sheet 110. Outdoor Leisure Dark Peak.

The Derwent Watershed has been described as the 'best, boggiest, bleakest, roughest, toughest, loneliest and wettest parts of the Peak District all brought into a day's walk encircling the headwaters of a fine river.' (Phil Cooper, *The Big Walks*, Diadem). So many superlatives might sound extravagant to the uninitiated, but no-one acquainted with this High Peak classic would argue the point!

If intending to hike the Derwent Watershed in one prolonged push, you will need plenty of daylight hours: sometime between May and August would fill the bill, though even then you may start or finish in darkness. That may not be as dicey as it sounds because an hour or two either side of the start involves the most straightforward terrain with less risk of going badly astray. You will also need a great deal of stamina and resourcefulness, and possibly someone to back up your attempt with food, drink and moral support at points along the way.

Although of identical length to that famous North York Moors challenge, the Lyke Wake Walk, in my view the Derwent Watershed is a significantly tougher proposition: trackless in places, it traverses upland terrain as rough and as tiring as anywhere in Britain. Given good weather, however, you will find this 'grand tour' of the Dark Peak rewarding on many levels—from the savage beauty of its wild places to the insights you will undoubtedly gain into your own abilities and disposition.

The River Derwent and its tributaries drain the High Peak moors whose prodigious rainfall is gathered in a chain of reservoirs serving the needs of adjacent industrial conurbations. Yorkshire Bridge, where inhabitants of the flooded valley settlements were rehoused and where the walk begins, lies downstream from Ladybower Reservoir; last to be built, it also claimed a good part of the Woodlands Valley to the west.

'Classic' walks in this book cover all the

Above: **Sunset from the Great Ridge near Mam Nick.**

Below: **Bleaklow sprawls along the western horizon—a view from Margery Hill on the Derwent Watershed walk.**

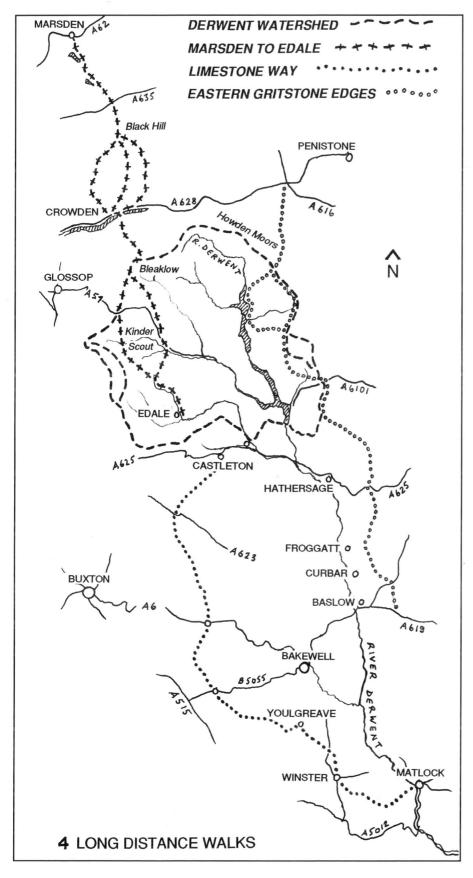

Map Legend

DERWENT WATERSHED – – – –

MARSDEN TO EDALE + + + + +

LIMESTONE WAY • • • • • • •

EASTERN GRITSTONE EDGES ○○○○○○○

4 LONG DISTANCE WALKS

Derwent Watershed ground except for the following stretches, each around 2 or 3 miles (3 to 5km) in length: the Snake Path to Devil's Dyke via Mill Hill and Moss Castle; Bleaklow Head to Swains Head; Margery Hill to Abbey Brook; and Dovestone Tor to Moscar via Strines Edge. In fact, the precise watershed is skirted here and there to give a more flowing line to the walk and to avoid some of the least rewarding ground.

Whether you set out in a clockwise or anti-clockwise direction provides food for thought at the planning stage. Clockwise you tackle first the hillier section over Win and Lose hills, the Great Ridge and Kinder; anti-clockwise you dispose of the remote and largely trackless Howden Moors while still fresh. My own preference is clockwise and that is how the route is described below.

The initial pull up to Win Hill is wooded and unrelenting—a cruel introduction—but the summit panorama more than compensates. A descent to cross the River Noe, at the gateway to the Vale of Edale just north of Hope, is followed by another substantial climb to the shapely top of Lose Hill, then an undulating ridge over Back Tor to much-visited Mam Tor—the 'Shivering Mountain' after its precipitously eroded east face. Rushup Edge culminates in Lord's Seat, beyond which the firm paths which hitherto have speeded progress give way to wetter going over Colborne to the trig pillar on Brown Knoll and thence to Edale Cross where you join the well defined alternative Pennine Way routing.

Kinder's western edge leads easily along to the famous Downfall, but purists will strike off north-east from Kinder Low across the hag-ridden plateau to its indeterminate 'summit' at 2088ft (636m) and on to Crowden Head (2070ft—631m) before swinging north-west to Ashop Head.

From the intersection with the Snake Path, the route remains coincident with the Pennine Way over Moss Castle and a frustrating maze of boggy groughs to reach the A57 Snake Road at its highest point between Sheffield and Manchester. Devil's Dike, Hern Clough and the Wain Stones mark your upward course to the wastes of Bleaklow Head (2060ft—628m) where Pennine Wayfarers veer thankfully west into Longdendale and you embark upon the loneliest—and for many the most testing—leg of the Watershed walk. But whatever adversity may lie ahead is counterbalanced by an overwhelming spaciousness and freedom from the treadmill of more populated paths and tracks. Here, unbridled nature will sharpen your senses and lift your spirits, though a careful eye must be kept on map and compass.

Walking east now, the way over Bleaklow

This traverse of the Dark Peak must rank as the best known of all Peak challenge walks. Its history pre-dates the National Park and has in common with the evolution of rock climbing the pre-World War I emergence of a new spirit of adventurism among industrial workers who looked to the hills for release from squalor and toil. The walk was introduced by Cecil Dawson, a Manchester cotton merchant and dedicated rambler, whose bog-trotting exploits in those early years of the twentieth century are remarkable even by today's standards.

The lure of traversing such potentially hostile country may seem hard to fathom for those as yet unfamiliar with the High Peak's perverse character. Perverse it is, because while conditions on the tops can be nightmarish, there is also strange, severe beauty to be found. In no way picturesque, such wild and weather-beaten places are sought by hillwalkers everywhere as a refuge from the shackles of mundanity and the constricting horizons of urban existence.

There is an appealing simplicity to the route: the line it takes crosses three high plateaux and its length falls within the range of a day's outing, albeit an intimidatingly hard one for the majority of walkers. Furthermore, it may be tackled at any time of year when conditions are favourable—snow and ice can bestow positive advantages by freezing boggy ground, though due regard must be paid to the weather outlook and hours of daylight. It is run annually as a fell race which produces fierce competition and finishing times of under 4 hours; equally, it has attracted the usual crop of double walks and extensions, but individuals could as easily take a couple of days to enjoy it, overnighting at Crowden.

From the hospitable little town of Marsden, once busy with cotton mills, a rough road heads south beside the four Wessenden Valley reservoirs. It is an oft-tramped track, being a Pennine Way rough-weather alternative for hikers dispirited by the horrors of Black Hill! Beyond Wessenden Lodge, with some 8 uninhabited miles (13km) in prospect ahead, the way crosses feeder streams and reaches the A635 Holmfirth to Mossley road at Wessenden Head.

Along to the right, a gate leads you onto the eroded, soggy flanks of Black Hill, the ascent of which will please only masochists! Soldiers

Hill to Bleaklow Stones—extraordinary, wind-sculpted gritstone boulders—is punctuated by occasional parish boundary stakes. Grinah Stones beckon a mile to the east, but halfway there you curve left round Swains Greave, source of the River Derwent itself. The ensuing stretch over the Howden Moors is generally considered to be the walk's crux: the odd boundary post will confirm navigation, but underfoot conditions can be heartbreaking—an apparent infinity of bog and peat groughs.

At Outer Edge trig pillar (1776ft—541m) difficulties relent and you cross the prominent Cut Gate track to mount Margery Hill, at 1791ft (546m) the highest spot in South Yorkshire. Unfortunately, yet more arduous terrain lies in store for those battling with a one-day circuit, and personal resources will be sorely tested. Once again, paths are a forgotten luxury as you struggle through deep, knee-wrenching tussocks of heather and coarse moorland grasses peppered with marshy hollows round the head of Abbey Brook.

At Back Tor the worst is over for, although still exposed to the elements, you are back in the realm of defined footpaths and stony sur-

faces. Some walkers opt to descend the Foulstone Delf bridleway from Back Tor to take advantage of the pub, thereafter reaching Moscar by minor road. Purists will tackle the (pathless!) traverse of Strines Edge. Either way, final southerly progress is made along the rocky escarpment of Stanage Edge to High Neb where any of several paths down through bracken will lead you to wooded Dennis Knoll and a tarmac descent back to Yorkshire Bridge.

Marsden to Edale

Start: Marsden.
Finish: Edale.
Access: Marsden lies 2 miles (3km) east of the A62 Oldham to Huddersfield road. Edale is reached by minor road from Hope, on the A625 Sheffield to Chapel-en-le-Frith road. Both termini have railway stations.
Distance: 21 to 25 miles (34 to 40km)—depending on route taken—10 to 12 hours
Terrain: Rough and boggy in places over 3 extensive plateaux above 2000ft (610m); especially arduous in bad weather.
Maps: OS Landranger Sheet 110. Outdoor Leisure Dark Park.

Lump, a trig-station established in 1784 by the Corps of the Royal Engineers, marks the oozing summit and a choice of three onward options: the Pennine Way path down by Crowden Great Brook; a more direct southerly line to Crowden over Tooleyshaw Moss, Westend Moss and Hey Edge; or (for speed and safety in bad weather) an easterly side-step to the A6124 moor road near Holme Moss television mast and an hour's tarmac bash to Woodhead.

Having attained the Longdendale Valley and crossed Skew Bridge, loins must be girded up for the 1400ft (427m) ascent and traverse of Bleaklow—no easy options here! At first, gritstone edges conceal its higher reaches (which you will have previewed from the recent descent) and the attack is mounted up by the Rollick Stones and Wildboar Clough. At Bleaklow Head (2060ft—628m) the Pennine Way is rejoined, though paths as such hardly exist in this desert of peat dunes and drainage channels.

Down beyond the heads of Hern and Crooked cloughs, Devil's Dike leads to the A57 Snake Pass and another choice of route. Purists will strike south over tussock grass and bilberry to Featherbed Moss and down through Upper Gate Clough before making the last uphill push over Black Ashop Moor and onto the Kinder escarpment edge. Others may prefer to diverge from the Pennine Way on Alport Low, enter Upper North Grain and drop into the Lady Clough Forest Trail to the Snake Inn, climbing thereafter into Gate Side Clough and onto the Kinder edges at Seal Stones.

Either via Fair Brook, or further east on the '7-minute crossing', the heavily dissected Kinder plateau is put behind you—in mist rather more easily said than done!—and a final descent made into Grindsbrook Clough. The Pennine Way, whose course has been shadowed, if not actually followed, throughout much of the walk, will take you easily to Edale village and, depending on your time of arrival, the welcome prospect of refreshment. It will have been well earned.

The Eastern Gritstone Edges

Start: Robin Hood Inn.
Finish: Flouch Inn.
Access: Robin Hood Inn lies 2 miles (3km) east of Baslow on the A619 from Chesterfield; nearest railway stations—Grindleford and Chesterfield. Flouch Inn lies at the crossroads of the A628 and A616 about 4 miles (6.5km) west of Penistone; nearest railway station—Penistone.
Distance: 27 miles (43km)—10 to 12 hours of walking.
Terrain: A series of high gritstone edges bearing good, firm paths but interrupted by

Above: **Curbar Edge—one link in the long chain of gritstone escarpments that stretch from Chatsworth north to the Flouch Inn.**

Below: **A welcome brew-up on a winter hike from Marsden to Edale.**

stretches of mixed ground. 4 miles (6.5km) of remote, trackless and very rough going between Back Tor and the Cut Gate track on the Howden Moors.

Maps: OS Landranger Sheets 119 and 110. Outdoor Leisure White Peak and Dark Peak.

Edges of millstone grit, in places high and wall-like, outcrop along a series of escarpments right down the east side of the National Park from Langsett almost to Matlock. It is not a continuous cliff barrier, neither are all the edges of imposing stature, but linked together they form a hike of immense character. Except towards the northern end of the route, walking is straightforward, navigation being rendered simpler than usual by one's need to follow the rocky edges themselves. However, you are aloft for most of the time and therefore exposed to the weather, more especially during the second half which is generally tougher than the first. Any overnight halt would have to utilise accommodation possibilities at Hathersage or Bamford since the moors beyond are devoid of habitation. Also, apart from a couple of hostelries half a dozen miles (10km) from the start, pubs and cafes stand well off-route, so adequate food and drink must be carried along with other requisites for tackling a major walk of this kind.

From the Robin Hood car park you set off north along Birchen Edge, a modest affair topped by a meagre obelisk known as Nelson's Monument. Where the rocks decline, open ground leads you ahead to the A621 then west on the old Chesterfield road (now a track) to the far more impressive Wellington's Monument.

Baslow, Curbar and Froggatt edges—a rock-climbers' mecca—give fast, easy going above the pastoral Derwent valley; from time to time it is worth wandering over to peer down the gritstone buttresses and perhaps watch climbing in progress.

Arrival at the Grouse Inn heralds a more sedate interlude through the grounds of Longshaw Country Park. From the A625 (the Fox House Inn is only a short distance to the east), the Duke of Rutland's Drive ascends to the head of the Burbage Brook valley and provides good views from below of Burbage Rocks, access along the crest being unavailable.

Another moor road linking Sheffield with the Derwent valley villages is crossed and soon you are striding out above some of the finest edge scenery of all. Stanage Edge is renowned for its climbing routes and extends north in a great arc past High Neb trig. pillar to Moscar. If you take to the under-edge path you will enjoy quite different perspectives: the choice is yours.

From Moscar you could strike north-east along Strines Edge to meet Derwent Edge at Dovestone Tor, but the path is indistinct and you miss several interesting rock formations. Instead the way heads west from Moscar House up the dip slope and swings north along Derwent Edge escarpment past the Wheel Stones (or Coach and Horses), the Salt Cellar and Cakes of Bread—the principal groups of wind-sculptured boulders and outcrops high above Ladybower Reservoir.

At Back Tor (1765ft—538m), you must change gear both physically and mentally. If unsure about relinquishing the good paths encountered thus far for some of the roughest ground in the entire Peak District, it might be advisable to descend via Lost Lad to Abbey Bank, walk up the reservoir road to Slippery Stones and climb Cut Gate to where you would otherwise have joined it north of Margery Hill. Mileage and ascent are increased, of course, but there is little likelihood of route-finding difficulties, particularly in foul weather.

A tentative trod leaves north-north-east from Back Tor, aiming for the headwaters of Abbey Brook. Here you swing north then north-west over Middle Moss—a trackless waste of ankle-twisting, strength—sapping moor—which temporarily contradicts the nature of this gritstone trail. However, veering north after a mile or two, there appears an edge to follow once again (though a less pronounced one), culminating in Margery Hill, at 1791ft (546m) South Yorkshire's highest top.

Maintaining the same direction for a further 400m or so brings you to an intersection with the unmistakable Cut Gate track, once in frequent use by Derwent valley farmers on their way to Penistone market, but now neglected by all except the walking fraternity. It meanders north-east for a mile then begins to drop along the landslipped Mickleden Edge above a beck of the same name, finally passing to the right of Hingcliff Hill and down to cross the Porter (or Little Don) river at Brook House Bridge. Less than a mile now from journey's end, you climb the western edge of a conifer plantation and reach the Flouch Inn at a busy crossroads 950ft (290m) above sea level.

The Limestone Way

Start: Matlock Bridge.
Finish: Castleton.
Access: Matlock Bridge lies just outside the south-east boundary of the National Park; nearest railway station—Matlock. Castleton is in the Hope Valley, on the A625 midway between Sheffield and Manchester; nearest railway station—Hope.

Distance: 26 miles (42km)—either attempted in one challenging go by strong walkers, or spread over 2 or more days by the less experienced.
Terrain: A varied course over the White Peak plateau past typical Peakland villages. All kinds of terrain involved, from rocky or muddy paths to farm tracks and country lanes. Numerous ups and downs.
Maps: OS Landranger Sheets 110 and 119. Outdoor Leisure White Peak.

This entertaining hike was initiated by West Derbyshire District Council and officially opened by Councillor F.W. Glossop at Matlock Town Hall on 8th May 1986 (The Council would like to receive comments about the route—send to The Limestone Way, Town Hall, Bank Road, Matlock, Derbyshire DE4 3NN).

The walk is well signposted and sets out to introduce walkers to the diverse nature of the limestone plateau: dramatic uplands overlaid by an ancient matrix of green lanes and drystone walls; the sheltered intimacy of dales; Peakland villages with their old cottages and welcoming pubs; relics from our industrial past and sites of even greater antiquity; and man's all-pervading influence on the land through his farming activity—a legacy dating back many centuries.

As well as exploring some of the lesser known dales in the north of the White Peak, this walk also presents a dramatic transformation in scenery towards the latter stages as you approach the geological boundary with Dark Peak gritstone. Contrasts there could hardly be drawn more sharply—especially in winter—as the enclosed horizons of limestone valleys are exchanged for open prospects of high moors.

Route complications along the way are few owing to the presence of waymarking. You could walk in either direction but I recommend a south to north journey for there is a greater likelihood of having the wind at your back.

Matlock is a multi-centred Victorian town set in a gorge on the River Derwent and extending 2 miles (3km) south from Matlock Bank to Matlock Bath, the 'tourist' end. Indeed, the Information Centre there will answer all your queries and is situated not far from the youth hostel and the Heights of Abraham cable-car. However, it is from near the railway station at Matlock Bridge that the Limestone Way begins.

You start by taking the Winster road and in 100m turning left up to Masson Hill and Bonsall, an old lead mining village built in two parts on steep hillside. At Upper Town you take to field tracks past Brumlea Farm, entering the National Park boundary west of Bright-gate and continuing via Luntor Rocks and Wyn's Tor to Winster, whose famous sixteenth-century Market Hall and other imposing buildings will attract your attention.

Peveril Castle and Cave Dale on the Limestone Way near Castelton.

Islington and Dudwood lanes lead on to Harthill Moor and the curious gritstone outcrop of Robin Hood's Stride, often used by rock-climbing beginners. Undulating field paths are then followed north-west to Youlgreave where a youth hostel, other accommodation, shops and refreshment places might suggest an overnight halt if you started late from Matlock 8 miles (12.5km) back.

Below Youlgreave the River Bradford runs through a wooded valley and the riverside path takes you pleasantly along to a fish-weir and

bridge where you turn up right, cross the Middleton road, pass Lomberdale Hall (once the home of Thomas Bateman, a local archaeologist) and emerge on the plateau at Moor Lane.

Over to Calling Low Farm and down pasture fields beyond, you dip down and up through Cales Dale to One Ash Grange with a camping barn loft—a possible stopping point at $11\frac{1}{2}$ miles (18.5km) for those equipped to use the basic accommodation offered. Your onward route to the halfway point at Moneyash is well walked and a north-west course is maintained thereafter to the remote hamlet of Flagg, with its fine Elizabethan Hall. At Town Head you swing north-east over gently rising ground and drop to the long, sloping village street at Taddington, another delightful Peakland settlement, blessed with a by-pass for the busy A6 which once ran through its centre.

Beyond Priestcliffe you descend sharply to Miller's Dale, taking Green Lane north to Peter Dale, one of a sequence of shallow dry valleys giving sheltered walking. Hay Dale is next, then Dam Dale and a jink up to the right to Hernstone Lane Head where the A623 climbs in a hairpin bend.

East of Peak Forest you cross Cop Round and will have become aware of a change in the countryside: surroundings are more open and austere and as you traverse Old Moor, peppered with old lead mines, there are exciting views ahead of the Great Ridge and the moors above Edale.

The walk's final stage lies through Cave Dale and down past Peveril Castle to Castleton, centre for the renowned Blue John show caves. Youth hostel, campsite and all other amenities exist here, and Hope railway station is little over 2 miles (3km) away. However, by extending the route by a further hour's hike north over Hollins Cross you could complete the transition from White to Dark Peak by ending at Edale, gateway to the gritstone moors and a very different kind of walking experience.

Useful Addresses

British Mountaineering Council
Crawford House
Booth Street East
MANCHESTER M13 9RZ

Camping & Caravanning Club of Great Britain
11 Lower Grosvenor Place
LONDON SW1W 0EX

Countryside Commission
John Dower House
Crescent Place
CHELTENHAM GL50 3RA

Council for National Parks
45 Shelton Street
LONDON WC2H 9HJ

Long Distance Walkers Association
c/o Kevin Uzzell
7 Ford Drive
Yarnfield
STONE
Staffs ST15 0RP

Losehill Hall
Peak National Park Study Centre
CASTLETON
Derbyshire S30 2WB

National Trust
36 Queen Anne's Gate
LONDON SW1H 9AS

(Peak District Regional Office:
Clumber Park Stableyard
WORKSOP S80 3BE)

Nature Conservancy Council
Northminster House
PETERBOROUGH PE1 1UA

(Peak District Regional Office:
Riverside House
Dale Road North
Darley Dale
MATLOCK DE4 2HX)

Peak District National Park
Aldern House
Baslow Road
BAKEWELL DE4 1AE

Ramblers Association
1/5 Wandsworth Road
LONDON SW8 2LJ

Royal Society for the Protection of Birds
The Lodge
SANDY
Bedfordshire SG19 2DL

Woodland Trust
Autumn Park
Dysart Road
GRANTHAM
Lincolnshire NG31 6LL

Youth Hostels Association
Trevelyan House
ST. ALBANS
Hertfordshire AL1 2DY

National Park Information Centres

BAKEWELL—tel (062981) 3227; closed winter Thursdays.
CASTLETON—tel (0433) 20679; open Easter to October and winter weekends.
DERBYSHIRE BRIDGE, GOYT VALLEY—open Sundays and Bank Holidays, Easter to September.
EDALE FIELDHEAD INFORMATION CENTRE—tel (0433) 70207; open daily 9.00 to 5.30.
FAIRHOLMES, DERWENT VALLEY—open Easter to September and October weekends.
HARTINGTON OLD SIGNAL BOX—open weekends and Bank Holidays, Easter to September.
TORSIDE, LONGDENDALE VALLEY—open weekends and Mondays, Easter to September.